S0-FJP-097

Table of Contents

PREFACE

This bibliography is a professional reference and resource guide for social workers, therapists, and researchers working with men who batter. It cites a broad selection of books and papers on the subject of men who batter, and provides an annotated listing of batterer program aids and manuals.

This comprehensive bibliography has several practical uses. One, it can help you maintain an appreciation of the dimensions of the discourse in our field——the concepts and issues being discussed. Two, it is an aid to investigating, in depth, a particular aspect or topic facing you in your work. Three, it can help broaden your knowledge of the field by providing a general survey of representative writings.

This bibliography should also prove particularly useful to students, and professionals entering the field from related specialties. With the increased awareness of wife abuse; family service agencies, police, mental health services, and alcohol and drug programs are also beginning to deal with the batterer. This bibliography provides a means to orient them to the issues and demands of working with batterers.

Introducing the bibliography is a critical overview of the research on batterers, a summary of some of the new knowledge and its limitations. Research on men who batter has rapidly expanded in the last five years and crossed into related fields like alcohol abuse, sexual assault, and aggression studies. It has challenged and refined many of our earlier speculations about men who abuse their wives. Also, research has raised new issues and questions to address in our work with batterers.

Following the overview, nearly 1,000 listings are organized within six major categories and 45 subcategories suggesting a structure for the field. The six major categories include research on wife battering, the roots of wife battering, research on the batterer, intervention with the batterer and program resources.

The first two categories list selected references on the background of wife abuse research and the social and cultural analysis that underlies it. Although the crisis orientation and practical concerns of most social services often preempt these fundamental conceptions, they are very much a part of the broader picture.

The next two categories are devoted to the batterer, and programs to stop his violence. This material is of the most immediate use and interest to the practitioner. While suggesting a range of interpretations and limited findings, it also broadens the possibilities of research and intervention.

Lastly, annotated program resources are listed. These resources reflect some of the progress that has been made in developing materials and organizational networks to help sustain and expand the work with batterers.

Admittedly, the review essay and especially the categorization reflect my own biases and interests. They do, nevertheless, attempt to acknowledge the diverse and often opposing emphases, approaches, and perspectives. Their inclusion does NOT mean to suggest my endorsement. But I do concede that there is still much to weigh and sort in what remains an emerging field. While we can be encouraged by the conscientious and ambitious research efforts, we still have to be cautious about our study and treatment of batterers. The harsh and well-documented reality is that the lives of many women and children are at stake.

My own work, as a clinical services researcher at the *Western Psychiatric Institute and Clinic* and as a group counselor of the *Second Step Program* for batterers in Pittsburgh, continues to influence my own orientation. I tend to view battering as rooted in our societal conceptions of men and women. While there are mediating psychological and familial factors, men abuse women in response to their conceptions of manhood. Abuse may be seen as a means, unconscious or not, of controlling and dominating one's wife or lover.

Ultimately, it is this belief system that must be *treated*, within and without, for individual men to stop their abuse and stay stopped.

Therefore, I have devoted much of my work to understanding and facilitating the change process in men who batter.

I am convinced that the most appropriate intervention is men's programs that promote long-term social support and monitoring while addressing the batterers' conceptions of masculinity——encouraging men to take responsibility for their own behavior. But clearly any one program cannot do it alone. A program must align itself with a larger community and societal effort for change.

Edward W. Gondolf

May 15, 1987

Overview of
Research on Men Who Batter

Fewer than five years ago Maria Roy (1982:33), speaking to several researchers in domestic violence, lamented the dearth of research on the batterer: "Recently, there has been a growing body of research on battered partners which has described their special unmet needs and suggested possible solutions. However, studies on the abusive partners are practically nonexistent to date, though the need to understand the problem of violent partnership as a whole is great." Since that time there has been an outpouring of studies of the characteristics of the batterer and interventions.

This development stems primarily from the preceding ten years of activism by feminists and shelter workers (Schechter, 1982). The battered women's movement helped confront the public with the horrors of wife battering, and established nearly 1,000 shelters and *safe homes* across the country. The care for and study of battered women brought with it stinging accounts of sadistic men and apologetic lovers (Martin, 1976; Walker, 1979). More systematic studies of the battered women and their reports of the batterers suggested a violence-prone man rather than a victim-prone woman (Bowker, 1983; Walker, 1984; Pagelow, 1981).

In other words, the batterer had to be restrained and changed if wife batterings were to be contained. Those studying battered women made appeals to address the batterer more directly (Fleming, 1979; Walker, 1979). But to do so required a better understanding of the batterer and ways to intervene effectively.

Since then, nearly 100 programs treating the batterer have emerged (Pirog-Good and Stets-Kealey, 1985), along with at least 20 states carrying out mandatory or "probable cause" arrest policies. Many of the batterer programs, therefore, also accept court referrals. The programs have increased access to "research subjects" who were previously elusive: the perpetrators of abuse.

The following discussion is an effort to critically summarize this new wave of research and outline the issues that remain. The overview begins by considering the social roots of battering and then the characteristics of the batterer. The diversity and performance of treatment programs for batterers are discussed next, followed by a look at the trends and issues of police intervention.

In sum, the number of studies on the characteristics of batterers in treatment and evaluations of batter programs has notably increased. There is, however, still much we do not know about batterers not in treatment and about the long-term impact of treatment. We must, therefore, continue to proceed with much caution to assure the safety of the battered women and their children.

THE ROOTS OF BATTERING

Researchers, clinicians and activists have forcibly argued that institutionalized sexism and violence in society at large is at the root of wife abuse. Feminists, in particular, have argued that male oppression, fear, and even hatred of women are manifest in wife abuse, as they are in rape and sexual harassment (Dobash and Dobash, 1979; Russell 1985). Several studies examining the relationship between factors like family power (Hauser, 1981), status (Hornug et al., 1981) or decision-making (Straus et al., 1980) and severity of abuse suggest that a complex but clear association is present. Cross-cultural (Bowker, 1985; Tellis-Nayak and Donoghue, 1982) and state comparisons (Yllo, 1983) do show less abuse occurring when greater opportunity is afforded to women.

Other social scientists have emphasized the expedient role of violence which is passed down from generation to generation (Stacey and Shupe, 1983, Straus et al., 1980). Several studies of intergenerational transmission reveal a high association between experiencing abuse as a child and being in a violent family as an adult (Bernard and Bernard, 1983; Kalmuss, 1984); even though others refute it (Dobash and Dobash, 1979; Pagelow, 1982).

This learned violence extends to both men and women, according to some researchers. Consistent with this theme, the most recent national incidence study (Straus and Gelles, 1986) asserts that too little attention has been given to the violence of women in relationships. Other studies counter with evidence that suggests mutual combat (Pagelow, 1985) is minimal and women's violence is largely in self-defense (Pleck et al., 1978; Saunders 1986).

The problem is that sound empirical data for the link between wife battering and societal processes, norms and structures is difficult to obtain. Establishing how social structure affects individual actions is a troublesome problem throughout the social sciences today. As the review essays of the research on wife abuse attest, we are thus left with inconclusive evidence for the prevailing theoretical explanations and clinical assumptions (Hotaling and Sugarman, 1986; Schumm et al., 1982).

This is not to dismiss our theories and assumptions but to refine them and improve our research methods. Most significantly, our research has been limited by small samples, questionable assessment instruments, unstated biases or the absence of fundamental theory (Breines and Gordon, 1983; Hart, 1984; Wardell, 1983). Research on wife battering may benefit by borrowing from and collaborating with parallel fields of research, as it is beginning to do (Fagan and Wexler, 1987).

BATTERER CHARACTERISTICS

The study of batterers in treatment has led to a refinement of the batterer profile: traditional sex roles attitudes, little impulse control, and poor communication skills (Coleman, 1980). Several studies confirm that batterers as a group are distinguished by violent family backgrounds, an excessive use of alcohol, and threatened status. They also tend toward extremes of aggressiveness-passivity (Telch and Lindquist, 1984) and denial-avoidance, as in the *Dr. Jekyll and Mr. Hyde syndrome* (Bernard and Bernard, 1984).

Alcohol and drug abuse also have a prevalent role in reinforcing wife battering. While there have been studies that show no differences in alcohol abuse between batters and nonbatterers (Rosenbaum and O'Leary, 1981), more recent comparative studies suggest that batterers as a group are more alcohol dependent than nonbatterers (Van Hasselt et al., 1986). As many as 50-70 percent of batterers abuse alcohol, but as much as 40 percent of the time they do not batter under the influence. The violence, however, tends to be more severe when batterers are under the influence of alcohol. Alcohol provides the batterer with, as one researcher points out, another excuse for the abuse (Gelles, 1979).

One review of the research on batterers makes a case that there is no firmly established direct causal connection between violence in the family of origin, alcohol abuse, personality characteristics, and demographic variables (Edleson et al., 1985). The studies of batterer characteristics, for instance, focus on men who have been in batterer programs or mandated counseling. These select men do not necessarily represent batterers in general. Also, all the studies are retrospective. There are no longitudinal studies that determine whether the characteristics are antecedents or symptoms of battering. On the whole, the research represents a form of reductionism —measuring isolated variables and ignoring the context of battering (Edleson et al., 1985).

Most studies fail to identify the terror-filled environment maintained by batterers and focus on the separate incidents of physical abuse. They unwittingly imply to practitioners that if we effectively treat the batterer's psychological and behavioral deficiencies, or *isolate the deviance,* we can stop the abuse. Generally, reviews of domestic violence research lament a failure to address more substantial theoretical questions (see Gondolf, 1985a; Hotaling and Sugarman, 1985).

THE FAILED MACHO COMPLEX

Interestingly, attitude scales reveal that batterers tend to rate themselves lower in masculinity (LaViolette et al., 1984; Rosenbaum, 1986) and self-esteem than the norm (Goldstein and Rosenbaum, 1985; Neidig et al., 1986; Rouse, 1984). These findings present an unclear picture on the surface. They may in part be a reflection of the pervasive sexual inequality that leaves male abusers and non-abuser with similar outlooks (Hotaling and Sugarman, 1986).

The accounts of batterers suggest that they may not fit the stereotype *supermacho man.* Rather, they may be typified as "failed macho complex" (Gondolf and Hanneken, 1987). The men who batter, often because of family-of-origin or subculture experiences, see themselves as less than the masculine ideal of dominance and cool. So, they overcompensate by controlling the one they perceive threatens or exposes their insecurities: their wife or lover.

Wife battering is therefore related to a batterer's distorted sense of masculinity and must be addressed as part of a larger effort to create a *new man* (Taubman, 1985). The research and commentary on the male sex role suggest that the repressive and unattainable male role bears strain (Pleck, 1981) and hazards for men (Fasteau, 1974; Goldberg, 1976). But as others with an eye on the larger social structure counter, the role is not without rewards of power and privilege. These more than amply compensate for any distresses (Sattel, 1983: Marciano, 1986).

Spurred by the women's movement, men's liberation efforts emerged to support a move toward androgeny and social change. The more recent attention to men's issues (Kimmel, ed., 1987), however, has turned more toward exploring men's feelings (Astrachan, 1986; Baumli, 1982) and misunderstandings women have of men (Farrell, 1986).

In any case, batterers are more than anger-driven men who can solve their problems by controlling their anger. Angry outbursts often accompany their battering, but their anger is instrumental and expressive. It is another means to get what they want. Furthermore, the anger often serves as another excuse to dismiss responsibility for the abuse and blame the victim (Ptacek, 1984). Anger and battering combine as an expedient way to maintain the batterer's privilege and power in the family (Scanzoni, 1978, 1982).

While there has been a drive to establish a clinical and empirical batterer profile based on characteristics, some recent studies suggest batterers may be dissimilar in some aspects. Personality inventories for men in a treatment program revealed "no unitary batterer profile" (Hamberger and Hastings, 1986). The batterers exhibited several personality disorders and categorical differences in anger arousal and expression.

Another typology is based on shelter women's reports of their batterer's background, abuse, and antisocial behavior. Their reports showed a generally violent and sadistic category of batterers and a more sporadic and apologetic category of batterers exhibiting the so-called "honeymoon" phase in the cycle of violence (Gondolf, Forthcoming-b). This finding corroborates earlier identified severe antisocial personalities among generally violent batterers (Fagan, 1983).

In sum, while there may be some commonalities in a batterer's sense of masculinity, there may also be different types of batterers requiring different diagnoses and treatment approaches.

PROGRAM FORMAT

National surveys of men's programs have attempted to document the trend in batterer services (Eddy and Myers, 1984; Feazell at al., 1984; Pirog-Good and Stets-Kealey, 1985; Roberts, 1984). A national directory (RAVEN, 1986) has also been established showing over 150 programs treating batterers. Most programs, however, are under-staffed, poorly funded, and have high dropout rates and very little follow-up (Roberts, 1984; Pirog-Good and Stets-Kealey, 1985).

The existing programs employ, moreover, several treatment modalities, but a distinguishing set of counseling methods in common. The most recent surveys showed that 59 percent of the programs used multiple counseling formats with 17 different treatment approaches. One survey concluded that the "majority of batter programs and services have adopted something of a theoretical and methodological 'shotgun approach' to working with batterers" (Eddy and Myers, 1984).

Nevertheless, many different published program descriptions (Edleson, 1984; Gondolf, 1985c; Purdy and Nickle, 1981; Saunders, 1984; Sonkin, et al., 1985) identify a few major components in common. These components include *cognitive restructuring, communication skill-building, stress reduction,* and *sex-role resocialization.*

More programs are emerging in which anger control is central to treatment (Deschner, 1984; Sonkin et al, 1985; Neidig et al., 1985). This trend toward anger control, however, does not account for the fundamental social dimensions of the problem established in the literature (Gondolf, 1985a). One popular guide for therapists (Sonkin et al., 1985), for instance, begins with essays by two prominent spokespersons of the shelter movement. These essays refer repeatedly to *patriarchy.* Yet the treatment approach that follows explicitly proposes anger control treatment and concludes with an *exposé* of the general violence in society.

Furthermore, there is some concern that anger is not a prime cause of the batterer's abuse (Gondolf, 1985b). Concentrating on anger as a treatment may be counterproductive, especially with the more severe batterers (Gondolf and Russell, 1986). For one, batterers, characterized by denial, tend to use anger as an excuse for their violence. In doing so they extend their denial. Anger control also provides an expedient "quick fix," relieving the batterer of more substantial change or punishment.

Programs differ in format and organization, as well as treatment orientation. The prevalent organizational types include counseling under the auspices of mental health and family services, adjuncts to women's shelters, and self-help programs or anti-sexist collectives. The grassroots self-help programs emphasize an anti-sexist analysis and resocialization of the batterer. The family service programs tend to be more clinical and professionally oriented, emphasizing psychological assessment and anger management (Gondolf, 1985c; Mettger, 1982).

There appears to be an increasing number of family services and family counselors treating batterers and their victims. A growing number of articles in professional journals present descriptions of family service-type programs, based largely on family systems assumptions (Taylor, 1984; Neidig et al., 1985; Weidman, 1986; Weitzman and Dreen, 1982). These programs also generally include individual and couples counseling, plus separate support groups for men and women, and children.

Thus, contention has increased between the family service programs and the grassroots programs. The debate between these positions is illustrated in the published exchange between an advocate of family services (Neidig, 1984), who attempted to discredit the grassroots groups because of their lack of professionalism, and an advocate of separate men's programs (Edleson, 1984). The latter asserted the diversity of men's programs and the need to address primarily the violence instead of the relationship, as the family service programs tend to do. Moreover, feminists employing a society conflict analysis of abuse argue that couples counseling, used by family services, often implicates and endangers the woman with the naive notion that there is primarily a communication problem between the batterer and the victim (Bograd, 1984; Breines and Gordon, 1983).

PROGRAM PERFORMANCE

The proof, of course, is in the pudding. Unfortunately, evaluations of programs have been hampered by several limitations. The surveys of men's programs have relied largely on the self-reports of staff for performance results. The current evaluation studies of programs suffer from the absence of control groups, no comparisons of treatment approaches, limited measures of success, short-term follow-ups, and no study of the group process (Gondolf, 1987b).

According to national surveys, the main problems of batterer programs, regardless of type, are low recruitment and high dropout rates. One survey revealed that one-third to one-half of the batterers dropped out after the first session (Pirog-Good and Stets-Kealey, 1986). An evaluation of another program shows that over twice as many men inquire about the program than enroll in it. About 30 percent of those who enter drop out before the end of three months (Gondolf, 1987c). One of the nation's leading programs reports treating about 1000 men during a 10 year span of activity, fewer than 2 percent of the estimated number of batterers in its vicinity.

Evaluations of program outcomes are often ambiguous. Follow-up studies are problematic, especially with such an elusive population and the difficulty in assessing the men's access to a potential victim during the follow-up period. The evaluation studies that include a follow-up suggest that about 60 percent of the batterers who complete a program are nonviolent 10-12 months after the program. There is some indication, however, that verbal and emotional abuse may escalate during the counseling, and the "accomplishment" of nonviolence may be used for self-congratulations and manipulation (Gondolf, 1987c; Edleson et al., 1986).

It is difficult to determine, however, the degree to which pressure from the women, police, or other social services influences the change. About 40 percent of the men in one follow-up were not living with a woman for the duration of the follow-up. Batterers who called but did not participate in the program also showed a 30 percent reduction in abuse (Gondolf, 1984). In fact, we can assume that nearly one-third of the clients in treatment programs would change their behavior without treatment (Blane, 1977).

The most sophisticated evaluation to date illustrates some of the problems of evaluating programs (Dutton, 1986). The study follows a quasi-comparison group and a court mandated counseling group for up to three years, showing a 36 percent "success" rate judged by recidivism. The calculations accounted for recoveries that would have been made irrespective of the treatment and verification from the wives of the batterers.

This conscientious study admits to many caveats, however. There were differences between the groups in previous arrest rates, men who had been screened from the counseling, the deterrent effects of the long-term surveillance, and psychological abuses which were not considered. Moreover, if the success rate is calculated including the dropouts from the counseling program with those who completed the program, the outcome of the program would be comparable to the control group of "nonparticipants."

At the other extreme is a study that offers an unqualified and inflated picture of program performance (Shupe and Stacey, 1987). It reports on a follow-up of three Texas programs to argue for success and expansion of such programs. Unfortunately, conclusions are drawn from only 25 percent of the potential follow-up subjects (N=360), and the large portion of program dropouts are not weighed in the final analysis. Moreover, the study concludes by advocating a model program that is not supported by its local shelter nor state shelter coalition.

Evaluations of alcohol and depression treatment have similar short-comings (Edward et al., 1977). They generally show little difference in the outcome of treatment modalities and often show little improvement over non-treated groups. Psychotherapy studies suggest that the counselor's commitment, counselor-client relationships, and group process may be more influential than the treatment approach (Bordin, 1986). Also, social support studies show that the community contacts and social environment may be the crucial determinant in the change (Gottlieb, 1981; Brownell and Shumaker, 1984, 1985).

THE CHANGE PROCESS

This is not to say that the evaluations are fruitless. They offer at least some caution lights that we can follow, if no steady green lights. There is also in progress a more rigorous comparative outcome study that may reveal more substantial results (Edleson et al., 1987). It may, however, make more sense to investigate how batterers who *do* change *have* changed, much as one study of battered women recruited "success cases" of the formerly battered who had managed to stop the abuse. This approach not only circumvents many of the evaluation shortcomings, but is also less pathologically focused. It identifies the potential strengths that men need to exercise and develop, rather than focusing on their deficiencies.

Preliminary research with reformed batterers suggests a developmental process of change that goes well beyond our conventional notion of "treatment" (Adams, 1984: Gondolf and Hanneken, 1987). There is increasing theoretical support from other fields for a developmental process of change or recovery (Denzin, 1985). The change process implies that a series of progressive interventions are in order, rather than the expectation that one program or treatment approach is sufficient (Gondolf, Forthcoming-c).

Some men's programs have already established a phased sequence of interventions moving the batterer from an instructional class, to theme-centered discussion groups, to a support group, to community service (Long, 1987). Furthermore, the increasing evidence of different types of batterers may warrant programs integrating themselves with other mental health and criminal justice programs. Short-term treatment may not only be insufficient, causing increased frustration among staff, but may also bring false hopes and danger for women.

The outcome of batterer programs is also at issue because of funding requirements and the potential competition the programs pose to shelters (Morrison, 1982). It is widely held by shelter workers, and shown in at least one study (Gondolf, Under review-b), that the batterer's participation in counseling is the greatest factor in differentiating the shelter women who return to batterers from those who don't. Similarly, the greatest influence on whether a man stays in counseling and reduces his violence appears to be the determination of his wife to stop that abuse (Bowker, 1983; Gondolf, 1987c).

In other words, batterer programs that "don't work" are especially dangerous because they tend to draw women back to unreformed batterers. This is not to discourage our earnest efforts to deal with the batterers. We need a sense of determination and commitment to sustain and improve our work.

The research, while it offers some clarification about batterers, suggests that we have to proceed as if batterer programs were still very much laboratories. As in most laboratory research we have to be cautious about the unforeseen side-effects and continue to improve and explore rather than feel satisfied.

A preoccupation with what "works" may reflect a desire for a finished product that does not exist. Ultimately, it may make more sense to use batterer programs as a means to address larger social issues rather than to "fix" a few men.

POLICE INTERVENTION

The role of police intervention with batterers continues to increase but not without some questions being raised. Feminists have strongly argued for the criminalization of wife battering (Armstrong, 1983) and mandatory arrest of batterers (Humphreys and Humphreys, 1985). In the past, police have hesitated to arrest batterers because the victim was often reluctant to press charges (only about 3 percent of the cases), and because of their own biases about wife abuse. Police arrests in wife battering cases vary from 6 percent to 13 percent (see Berk and Newton, 1986).

The role of arrest in domestic violence incidents has therefore become the topic of several studies. The Minneapolis Police Study (Sherman and Berk, 1984) showed arrests, on the average, to be 20 percent more effective in reducing recidivism than mediating or forcing the batterers to leave. A replication of this field experiment, using police records, showed that a reduction in abuse is greatest for the batterers whom the police would ordinarily be inclined to arrest. In other words, the deterrent effect applies to a certain kind of batterer. Mandatory arrest may therefore be ineffective with batterers in general.

Arrests appear to hinge more on extra-legal or situational factors (whether the batterer was drinking, who contacted the police, and the victim's willingness to press charges), rather than on evidence that the law has been violated (Berk and Newton, 1986; Worden and Pollitz, 1984). The batterer's antisocial conduct (other arrests, alcohol abuse, and general violence) also strongly influences the police intervention process (Gondolf, Under review-c). However, in at least 20 percent of the cases reported by shelter women the batterers were not particularly antisocial, but still committed severe abuse. The police "did nothing" in these cases and thus drew more negative appraisals from the women (Gondolf, Under review-c).

For many battered women, involvement with the legal system is not a desirable outcome. Regardless of their fears of their husbands, their fears of the legal system are greater (Radford, 1987). As many as 20 states now have "probable cause" or mandatory arrests policies in which police must arrest the batterer regardless of the victim's intent to press charges. Arrest rates increased 25 fold in response to Ontario's mandatory arrest policy, rather than decreasing women's reporting or the number of cases heard in court, as feared (Jaffe et al., 1986). Unfortunately, police still exercise much discretion in implementing mandatory arrest. One study found the law unenforced in as many as 40 percent of the battering cases (Ferraro, 1985).

Moreover, some feminists have expressed second thoughts in that the "get tough" policy relegates abuse to a form of "deviance" separate from the "normal" population (Scales, 1986). It diverts attention from the goal of supplying the resources to women that would give them more mobility and opportunity, resources that would give women more control of their own lives and the ability to establish independence and safety (Ferraro, 1985).

Another problem is what to do with the batterers after releasing them from jail. A turn towards court mandated and diversion counseling is thus under way. While it makes sense to continue the intervention beyond arrest, court mandated counseling also may have its limitations if not well coordinated with the criminal justice system (Dutton, Forthcoming). It must also extend beyond anger control instruction.

Sometimes mandated counseling blunts the deterrence of arrest. In a practical sense, attending a twelve-week program is a small price to pay for years of abuse and harm. The rapid expansion of mandated counseling is also of concern given the significant proportion of severely antisocial and criminally-prone personalities involved in abuse. The batterer programs need to be cautious that they do not become dumping grounds for men that should be more forcibly restrained. Furthermore, other diversion programs for drunk driving or delinquency have shown that recidivism resumes after the standard follow-up of six months to a year (Cavaila, 1984).

CONCLUSION

All this seems to argue for a more coordinated series of interventions that promotes a long-term commitment to change. There is in our culture, however, a tendency toward "quick fix," high-tech solutions to difficult problems. Some of the research on wife battering suggests that we might also be unwittingly looking for such a solution in this field.

A more critical consideration of the research implies, on the other hand, that much soul searching is still in order, especially on the topic of batterers. There are several issues that remain largely unaddressed by the current research efforts. The overriding issue relates to safety. The question most frequently asked by shelter women and staff is, "When is it safe to return to the batterer?" We have no easy answer for this, and lethality predictions have been notoriously unreliable. What precautions are therefore necessary and effective? How do we better detect the potential for relapse, and what interventions are appropriate for it?

The field of alcohol treatment and recovery offers some indication that "relapse" can be anticipated and managed more effectively. It is still unclear how batterers change, but the evidence appears to suggest that their "staying stopped" is part of a long-term process. In this regard, how do we promote the long-term commitment to change that is as necessary for most batterers as it is for many alcoholics? Do some treatment approaches preempt this long-term process in favor of short-term results?

Several interventions are obviously needed to stop wife battering. Program evaluations may therefore need to consider the outcome of various combinations of interventions, rather than the outcome of a single programmatic intervention. What is the "outcome" for a batterer who is arrested, passed to an instructional program, and eventually into some sort of community service? What relation does sheltering of the woman have to the man's change? Can we better appraise the battered woman of the man's change process in a way that would better protect them and reinforce the changes?

We have furthermore virtually failed to address the diversity of batterers that is before us. Our programs have particularly low representations of black and Hispanic men. What can be done to assure their participation and change? Also, wife battering is often accompanied by child abuse, incest and marital rape. Should these abuses be addressed separately, or as part of a larger dynamic?

There is increasing evidence of multi-problem batterers, men with criminal records, severe alcohol abuse, and psychopathology. What additional or special treatment needs to be directed toward this particularly dangerous population of batterers? Is there a role for batterer programs within a residential setting, alcohol detox facility, or prison?

Finally, if wife battering is a deep-seated social problem, as so much of the field has asserted, how do we assure the resources and motivation to address its social roots? Is there any evidence that men's programs have a positive impact on the community at large? Perhaps the outcome measures for evaluation need to account for the impact on the community's perceptions of abuse and the deterrent effect on the huge number of batterers who never participate in a treatment program. How, too, do we increase community involvement in confronting and stopping the batterer? What's to be done, in particular, to enlist more men's service clubs, businesses, and sports teams in the effort to address the underlying causes of woman abuse and battering?

Given the embeddedness and extent of the problem, what we may need most is a sense of endurance and resiliency. How we muster and sustain that "spirit" may be the most elusive and most vital aspect to determine. It may be related in part to how we better support and nourish each other in a field that is often fraught with controversy and contention. Our relationship to the victims and victimizers also contributes to our spirit. Do we assume the posture of expert professionals attempting to diagnose and treat deviant cases, or that of facilitators and advocates with similar experiences and tendencies? In sum, our example, commitment, and outlook are essential ingredients in addressing wife abuse. They, too, deserve our personal and research attention if we are to further the progress charted here.

Dynamics of Wife Battering

— Wife Battering Books —

OVERVIEW OF FAMILY VIOLENCE

Armstrong, L. 1983. *The Home Front: Notes on the Family War Zone.* New York: McGraw-Hill.

Davidson, T. 1978. *Conjugal Crime: Understanding and Changing the Wifebeating Problem.* New York: Hawthorne.

Fleming, J. B. 1979. *Stopping Wife Abuse.* Garden City, NY: Anchor Books.

Freeman, M. 1979. *Violence in the Home.* Westmead, England: Saxon House.

Gelles, R. J. 1974. *The Violent Home: A Study of Physical Aggression Between Husbands and Wives.* Beverly Hills, CA: Sage.

Guberman, C., and M. Wolfe, eds. 1985. *Violence Against Women and Children.* Toronto, Canada: Women's Press.

Langley, R., and R. Levey. 1977. *Wife Beating: The Silent Crisis.* New York: Pocket Books.

Lystad, M., ed. 1986. *Violence in the Home: Interdisciplinary Perspectives.* New York: Brunner/Mazel.

Martin, D. 1976. *Battered Wives.* New York: Pocket Books.

McNulty, F. 1980. *The Burning Bed.* New York: Harcourt Brace Jovanovich.

Pagelow, M. D. 1984. *Family Violence.* New York: Praeger.

Pleck, E. 1987. *Domestic Tyranny: The Making of American Social Policy Against Family Violence From Colonial Times to the Present.* New York: Oxford University Press.

Stacey, W., and A. Shupe. 1983. *The Family Secret: Domestic Violence in America.* Boston: Beacon.

Straus, M. A., R. J. Gelles, and S. Steinmetz. 1980. *Behind Closed Doors: Violence in the American Family.* New York: Anchor/Doubleday.

U.S. Department of Justice. 1984. *Attorney General's Task Force on Family Violence: Final Report.* Washington, D.C.

STUDIES OF BATTERED WOMEN

Bowker, L. 1983. *Beating Wife Beating.* Lexington, MA: Lexington.

Browne, A. 1987. *When Battered Women Kill.* New York: Free Press.

Dobash, E. R., and R. Dobash. 1979. *Violence Against Wives: A Case Against the Patriarchy.* New York: Free Press.

Giles-Sims, J. 1983. *Wife Battering: A Systems Theory Approach.* New York: Guilford.

Okum, L. 1986. *Woman Abuse: Facts Replacing Myths.* Albany: State University of New York.

Pagelow, M. D. 1981. *Woman-Battering: Victims and Their Experiences.* Beverly Hills, CA: Sage.

Rhodes, D., and S. McNeil, eds. 1985. *Women Against Violence Against Women.* London: Onlywomen Press.

Schechter, S. 1982. *Women and Male Violence: The Visions and Struggles of the Battered Women's Movement.* Boston: South End Press.

Stanko, E. A. 1985. *Intimate Intrusions: Women's Experience of Male Violence.* Boston: Routledge & Kegan Paul.

Walker, L. 1979. *The Battered Women.* New York: Harper.

Walker, L. 1984. *The Battered Woman Syndrome.* New York: Springer.

RESEARCH ANTHOLOGIES

Finkelhor, D., R. Gelles, G. T. Hotaling, and M. A. Straus, eds. 1983. *The Dark Side of Families: Current Family Violence Research.* Beverly Hills, CA: Sage.

Hotaling, G. T., and M. A. Straus, eds. Forthcoming. *New Directions in Family Violence Research.* Beverly Hills, CA: Sage.

Johnson, N., ed. 1985. *Marital Violence.* Boston: Routledge & Kegan Paul.

Russel, G., ed. 1986. *Violence in Intimate Relationships.* New York: Spectrum Press.

Roy, M., ed. 1977. *Battered Women: A Psychosociological Study of Domestic Violence.* New York: Van Nostrand Reinhold.

Roy, M., ed. 1982. *The Abusing Partner: An Analysis of Domestic Battering.* New York: Van Nostrand Reinhold.

Straus, M. A., and G. Hotaling, eds. 1980. *The Social Causes of Husband-Wife Violence.* Minneapolis, MN: Univ. of Minnesota Press.

Yllo, K., and M. Bograd, eds. 1987. *Feminist Perspectives on Wife Abuse.* Beverly Hills, CA: Sage.

— Wife Battering Papers —

THEORY

Berk, R., S. F. Berk, D. Loseke, and D. Rauma. 1983. "Mutual Combat and Other Family Violence Myths." In D. Finkelhor et al., eds. *The Dark Side of Families.* Beverly Hills, CA: Sage.

Bern, E. H. 1985. "Domestic Violence: Some Theoretical Issues Related to Criminal Behavior." *Journal of Applied Social Sciences.* 1:136-147.

Carlson, B. E. 1984. "Causes and Maintenance of Domestic Violence: An Ecological Analysis." *Social Service Review.* 58(4): 569-587.

Denzin, N. 1985. "Towards a Phenomonology of Family Violence." *American Journal of Sociology.* 90(3): 483-513.

Dobash, E. R., and R. Dobash. 1981. "Social Science and Social Action: The Case of Wife Beating." *Journal of Family Issues.* 2:27-39.

Farrington, K. 1986. "The Application of Stress Theory to the Study of Family Violence: Principles, Problems, and Prospects." *Journal of Family Violence.* 1(2): 131-148.

Ferraro, K. 1984. "An Existential Approach to Battering." Paper presented at the Second National Conference for Family Violence Researchers, Durham, NH.

Gelles, R. J. 1981. "Theoretical Approaches to the Issue of Intrafamily Violence." *Behavior Therapy.* 5:5-8.

Gelles, R. J. 1983. "An Exchange/Social Control Theory." In D. Finkelhor et al., eds. *The Dark Side of Families.* Beverly Hills, CA: Sage.

Gelles, R. J., and M. A. Straus. 1979. "Determinants of Violence in the Family: Toward a Theoretical Integration." In W. Burr et al., eds. *Contemporary Theories About the Family.* New York: Free Press.

Gordon, L. 1986. "Family Violence, Feminism, and Social Control." *Feminist Studies.* 12:3.

Guerney, B. G., M. Waldo, and L. Firestone. In press. "Wife-Battering: A Theoretical Construct and Case Report." *American Journal of Family Therapy.*

Kratcoski, P. C. 1984. "Perspectives on Intrafamily Violence." *Human Relations.* 37(6): 443-453.

Lesse, S. 1979. "The Status of Violence Against Women: Past, Present, and Future Factors." *American Journal of Psychotherapy.* 33:190-200.

Levine, E. M. 1986. "Sociocultural Causes of Family Violence: A Theoretical Comment." *Journal of Family Violence.* 1(1): 3-12.

Lystad, M. 1986. "Interdisciplinary Perspective on Family Violence: An Overview." In M. Lystad, ed. *Violence in the Home: An Interdisciplinary Perspective.* New York: Brunner/Mazel.

Neidig, P. H., D. H. Friedman, and B. S. Collins. 1984. "Spouse Abuse: Mutual Combat or Wife Battering." Unpublished manuscript. Coastal Empire Mental Health Center, Beauford, SC.

Nichols, B. B. 1976. "The Abused Wife Problem." *Social Casework.* 57:27-32.

Straus, M. A. 1977. "A Sociological Perspective on the Prevention and Treatment of Wifebeating." In M. Roy, ed. *Battered Women.* New York: Van Nostrand Reinhold.

Straus, M. A. 1983. "Ordinary Violence, Child Abuse, and Wife-Beating: What Do They Have in Common?" In D. Finkelhor et al., eds. *The Dark Side of Families.* Beverly Hills, CA: Sage.

Studer, M. 1984. "Wife Beating as a Social Problem: The Process of Definition." *International Journal of Women's Studies.* 7(5): 412-422.

Wiggins, J. A. 1983. "Family Violence as a Case of Interpersonal Aggression: A Situational Analysis." *Social Forces.* 62(1): 102-123.

RESEARCH REVIEWS

Bagarozzi, D., and C. W. Giddings. 1983. "Conjugal Violence: A Critical Review of Current Research and Clinical Practices." *The American Journal of Family Therapy.* 11(1): 3-15.

Breines, W., and L. Gordon. 1983. "The New Scholarship on Family Violence." *Signs.* 8(3): 490-531.

Davis, L. V. 1987. "Battered Women: The Transformation of a Social Problem." *Social Work.* 32(4): 306-311.

Finkelhor, D. 1983. "Common Features of Family Abuse." In D. Finkelhor et al., eds. *The Dark Side of Families.* Beverly Hills, CA: Sage.

Flynn, J. 1977. "Recent Findings Related to Wife Abuse." *Social Casework.* 58(1): 13-20.

Frieze, I. H., and A. Browne. 1986. "Violence in Marriage." In L. Ohlin and M. H. Tonry, eds. *Crime and Violence.* Chicago: Jossey-Bass.

Geffner, R., S. K. Cook. 1986. "Recent Trends in Spouse Abuse and Family Violence Research." Paper presented at Violence in America Conference, Dallas, TX.

Hart, B. 1984. "What Every Researcher and Clinician Should Know About the Battered Women's Shelter Movement." Paper presented at the Second National Conference for Family Violence Researchers, Durham, NH.

Hotaling, G. T., and D. Sugerman. 1986. "An Analysis of Risk Makers in Husband to Wife Violence: The Current State of Knowledge." *Violence and Victims*. 1(2): 101-124.

Klein, F. 1983. "Violence Against Women." In B. Haber, ed. *The Women's Annual 1982-1983*. Boston: G. K. Hall.

Pfouts, J. H., and C. Renz. 1981. "The Future of Wife Abuse Problems." *Social Work*. 26(6): 451-455.

Schumm, W. R., J. J. Martin, S. R. Bolman, and A. P. Jurich. 1982. "Classifying Family Violence: Whither the Woozle." *Journal of Family Issues*. 3(3): 319-340.

Stahly, G. B. 1977. "A Review of Select Literature of Spousal Violence." *Victimology*. 2(3-4): 591-607.

Wardell, L., D. Gillespie and A. Leffler. 1983. "Science and Violence Against Wives." In D. Finkelhor et al., eds. *The Dark Side of Families*. Beverly Hills, CA: Sage.

INTERGENERATIONAL TRANSMISSION

Bernard, M. L., and J. L. Bernard. 1983. "Violent Intimacy: The Family as a Model for Love Relationships." *Family Relations*. 32:283-286.

Kalmuss, D. 1984. "The Intergenerational Transmission of Marital Aggression." *Journal of Marriage and the Family*. 47(1): 11-19.

Carroll, J. C. "The Intergenerational Transmission of Family Violence: The Long-Term Effects of Aggressive Behavior." *Advances in Family Psychiatry*. 2:171-181.

Owens, D., and M. A. Straus. 1975. "Social Structure of Violence in Childhood and Approval of Violence as an Adult." *Aggressive Behavior Journal*. 1:193-211.

Pagelow, M. D. 1982. "Violence In Families: Is There An Intergenerational Transmission?" Paper presented at Society for the Study of Social Problems, San Francisco, CA.

Peterson, R. 1980. "Social Class, Social Learning and Wife Abuse." *Social Service Review*. 54(3): 390-405.

Rosenberg, M. S. 1984. "The Impact of Witnessing Interparental Violence on Children: Implications for the Concept of Intergenerational Violence." Paper presented at the Second National Conference for Family Violence Researchers, Durham, NH.

POWER AND STATUS

Alder, E. M. 1981. "The Underside of Married Life: Power, Influence, and Violence." In L. H. Bowker, ed. *Women and Crime in America.* New York: Macmillan.

Allen, C. M., and M. A. Straus. 1985. "Final Say Measures of Marital Power." *Journal of Marriage and the Family.* 46(3): 619-630.

Bowker, L. H. 1985. "The Effects of National Development on the Position of Married Women in the Third World: The Case of Wife-Beating." *International Journal of Comparative and Applied Criminal Justice.* 9(1): 1-13.

Cazenave, N. A., and M. A. Straus. 1979. "Race, Class, Network Embeddedness and Family Violence: A Search for Potent Support Systems." *Journal of Comparative Family Studies.* 10(3): 281-299.

Gillespie, D. L. 1971. "Who Has the Power? The Marital Struggle." *Journal of Marriage and the Family.* 33:445-458.

Gondolf, E. W., E. R. Fisher, and R. J. McFerron. Forthcoming. "Racial Differences Among Shelter Residents: A Comparison of Anglo, Black and Hispanic Battered Women." *Journal of Family Violence.*

Goode, W. 1971. "Force and Violence in the Family." *Journal of Marriage and the Family.* 33(4): 624-636.

Hauser, W. J. 1981. *Difference in Relative Resources, Familial Power, and Spouse Abuse.* Palo Alto, CA: R & E Research Assoc.

Hornug, C. A., B. C. McCullough, and T. Sugimoto. 1981. "Status Relationship in Marriage: Risk Factors in Spouse Abuse." *Journal of Marriage and the Family.* 43:675-692.

Kalmuss, D. S. and M. A. Straus. 1982 "Wife's Marital Dependency and Wife Abuse." *Journal of Marriage and the Family.* 44(2): 277-286.

Kolb, T. M., and M. A. Straus. 1974. "Marital Power and Marital Happiness in Relation to Problem Solving Ability." *Journal of Marriage and the Family.* 36:756-766.

LaRossa, R. 1980. "And We Haven't Had Any Problems Since: Conjugal Violence and the Politics of Marriage. In M. A. Straus and G. T. Hotaling, eds. *The Social Causes of Husband-Wife Violence.* Minneapolis: Univ. of Minnesota Press.

Lockhart, L. L. 1985. "Methodological Issues in Comparative Racial Analysis: The Case of Wife Abuse." *Social Work Research and Abstracts.* 21(2): 35-41.

Metzger, M. 1978. "A Social History of Battered Women." *Heresies.* 6:58-68.

O'Leary, K. D., and A. D. Curley. 1986. "Assertion and Family Violence: Correlates of Spouse Abuse." *Journal of Marital and Family Therapy.* 12(3): 281-289.

Resick, P. A. 1983. "Sex Role Stereotypes and Violence Against Women." In V. Franks and E. D. Rothblum, eds. *The Stereotyping of Women: Its Effects on Mental Health.* New York: Springer.

Tauchen, H. V., K. Long, and A. D. Witte. 1983. "Economic Issues in Family Violence: Violence as a Control Mechanism." Unpublished paper, University of North Carolina, Chapel Hill.

Tellis-Nayak, V., and G. O'Donoghue. 1982. "Conjugal Egalitarianism and Violence Across Cultures." *Journal of Comparative Family Studies.* 13(3): 277-289.

Tidmarsh, M. 1976. "Violence in Marriage: The Relevance of Structural Factors." *Social Work Today.* 7(2): 36-48.

Yllo, K. 1983. "Sexual Equality and Violence Against Wives in American States." *Journal of Comparative Family Studies.* 14(1): 67-86.

INCIDENCE AND IMPACT

Bowker, L. H., M. Arbitell, and J. R. McFerron. In press. "On the Relationship between Wife-Beating and Child Abuse." In K. Yllo and M. Bograd, eds. *Feminist Perspectives on Wife Abuse.* Beverly Hills, CA: Sage.

Campell, J. C. 1985. "Beating of Wives: A Cross-Cultural Perspective." *Victimology.* 10(1-4): 174-185.

DeGregovia, B. 1987. "Sex Attitude and Perception of Psychological Abuse." *Sex Roles.* 16(5-6): 227-237.

Gelles, R. J. 1975. "Violence and Pregnancy: A Note on the Extent of the Problem and Needed Services." *Family Coordinator.* 24:1.

Hershorn, M., and A. Rosenbaum. 1985. "Children of Marital Violence: A Closer Look at the Unintended Victims." *American Journal of Orthopsychiatry.* 55(2): 260-266.

Hoffman, P. 1984. "The Psychological Abuse of Women by Spouses and Live-in Lovers." *Women and Therapy.* 3(1): 37-47.

Levine, E. M. 1975. "Interpersonal Violence and Its Effects on the Children: A Study of Fifty Families in General Practice." *Medicine, Science, and Law.* 15:172-175.

Liaboe, G. P. 1985. "The Place of Wife Battering In Considering Divorce." *Journal of Psychology and Theology.* 13(2): 129-138.

Margolin, G. 1987. "The Multiple Forms of Aggressiveness Between Marital Partners: How Do We Identify Them?" *Journal of Marital and Family Therapy.* 13(1): 77-84.

Mills, T. 1984. "Victimization and Self-Esteem: On Equating Husband Abuse and Wife Abuse." *Victimology.* 9(2): 254-261.

NSPCC School of Social Work. 1977. "Yo Yo Children: A Study of Two Violent Matrimonial Cases." In M. Roy, ed. *Battered Women.* New York: Van Nostrand Reinhold.

Pagelow, M. D. 1985. "The 'Battered Husband Syndrome': Social Problem or Much Ado About Little?" In N. Johnson, ed. *Marital Violence.* Boston: Routledge & Kegan Paul.

Pleck, E., J. Pleck, M. Grossman, and P. Bart. 1978. "The Battered Data Syndrome: A Reply to Steinmetz." *Victimology.* 2(3-4): 680-683.

O'Brien, J. E. 1971. "Violence in Divorce Prone Families." *Journal of Marriage and the Family.* 33(4): 692-698.

O'Leary, K. D. 1987. "Prevalence and Stability of Spousal Aggression." Paper presented at the Third National Family Violence Research Conference, Durham, NH.

Pfouts, J. H., J. H. Schapler, and H. C. Henly. 1982. "Forgotten Victims of Family Violence." *Social Work.* 27(4): 367-368.

Rosenbaum, A., and K. D. O'Leary. 1982. "Children: The Unintended Victims of Marital Violence." *American Journal of Orthopsychiatry.* 51(4): 692-699.

Saunders, D. G. 1977. "Marital Violence: Dimension of the Problem and Modes of Intervention." *Journal of Marriage and Family Counseling.* 3(1): 43-52.

Saunders, D. G. 1986. "When Battered Women Use Violence: Husband-Abuse or Self-Defense?" *Violence and Victims.* 1(1): 47-60.

Schwartz, M. D. 1987. "Gender and Injury in Spouse Abuse." *Sociological Focus.* 20(1): 61-75.

Snyder, D., and L. Fruchtman. 1981. "Differential Patterns of Wife Abuse: A Data-Based Typology." *Journal of Consulting & Clinical Psychology.* 49(6): 878-885.

Steinmetz, S. 1977. "Wifebeating, Husbandbeating: A Comparison of the Use of Physical Violence Between Spouses to Resolve Marital Fights." In M. Roy, ed. *Battered Women*. New York: Van Nostrand Reinhold.

Straus, M. A. 1986. "Societal Morphogenesis and Intrafamily Violence in Cross-Cultural Perspective." In R. J. Gelles and C. P. Cornell, eds. *International Perspectives on Family Violence*. Lexington, MA: Lexington.

Straus, M. A., and R. J. Gelles. 1985. "Societal Change and Change in Family Violence from 1975 to 1985 as Revealed by Two National Surveys." *Journal of Marriage and the Family*. 48:465-479.

Wasileski, M., M. E. Callaghan-Chaffee, and R. B. Chaffee. 1982. "Spousal Violence in Military Homes: An Initial Survey." *Military Medicine*. 147(9): 761-765.

Wolfe, D. A., J. Zak, S. K. Wilson, and P. Jaffe. 1986. "Child Witnesses to Violence between Parents: Critical Issues in Behavioral and Social Adjustment." *Journal of Abnormal Child Psychology*. 14(1): 95-101.

CONTRIBUTING FACTORS

Amato, P. R. 1986. "Marital Conflict, the Parent-Child Relationship and Child Self-Esteem." *Family Relations*. 35:403-410.

Bern, E. H. 1982. "From Violent Incident to Spouse Abuse Syndrome." *Social Casework*. 63(1): 41-47.

Barling, J., and A. Rosenbaum. 1986. "Work Stressor and Wife Abuse." *Journal of Applied Psychology*. 71(2): 346-348.

Brutz, J. L., C. M. Allen. 1986. "Religious Commitment, Peace Activism, and Marital Violence in Quaker Families." *Journal of Marriage and the Family*. 48:481-502.

Coleman, K. H., M. L. Weinman, and B. P. Hsi. 1980. "Factors Affecting Conjugal Violence." *Journal of Psychology*. 105:197-202.

Fergusson, D. M., L. J. Horwood, K. L. Kershaw, and F. T. Shannon. 1986. "Factors Associated with Reports of Wife Assault in New Zealand." *Journal of Marriage and the Family*. 48:407-412.

Gelles, R. J. 1977. "No Place to Go: The Social Dynamics of Marital Violence." In M. Roy, ed. *Battered Women*. New York: Van Nostrand Reinhold.

Goldberg, H. 1984. "The Dynamics of Rage Between the Sexes in a Bonded Relationship." In L. Barnhill, ed. *Clinical Approaches to Family Violence*. Aspen, CO: Aspen Family Therapy Series.

Hotaling, G. T., and D. Sugerman. 1986. "An Analysis of Risk Makers in Husband to Wife Violence: The Current State of Knowledge." *Violence and Victims.* 1(2): 101-124.

Kalmuss, D. S., and J. A. Seltzer. 1986. "Continuity of Marital Behavior in Remarriage: The Case of Spouse Abuse." *Journal of Marriage and the Family.* 48:113-120.

Linz, D. 1987. "Desensitization to Media Violence and Reactions to Victims of Battering." Paper presented at the Third National Family Violence Research Conference, Durham, NH.

Lewis, B. Y. 1987. "Psychosocial Factors Related to Wife Abuse." *Journal of Family Violence.* 2(1): 1-10.

Malamuth, N. M., and J. Briere. 1986. "Sexual Violence in the Media: Indirect Effects on Aggression Against Women." *Journal of Social Issues.* 42(3): 75-89.

O'Leary, K. D., and I. Arias. 1987. "Prevalence, Correlates, and Development of Spouse Abuse." In R. D. Peters and R. J. McMahon, eds. *Marriage and Families: Behavioral Treatments and Processes.* New York: Brunner/Mazel.

Resick, P. A., and D. Reese. 1986. "Perceptions of Family Social Climate and Physical Aggression in the Home." *Journal of Family Violence.* 1(1): 71-83.

Straus, M. A. 1974. "Leveling, Civility, and Violence in the Family." *Journal of Marriage and the Family.* 36:13-29.

Symonds, M. 1978. "The Psychodynamics of Violence-Prone Marriages."*American Journal of Psychoanalysis.* 38:213-222.

Wirtz, P. Forthcoming. "Psychological Response to Assaultive Characteristics of Abusive Couples." *Journal of Consulting & Clinical Psychology.* 49:63-71.

PREMARITAL ABUSE

Albritten-Bogal, R. B., and W. L. Albritten. 1985. "The Hidden Victims: Courtship Violence Among College Students." *Journal of College Student Personnel.* 26:201-204.

Arias, I., M. Samios, and K. D. O'Leary. 1987. "Prevalence and Correlates of Physical Aggression During Courtship." *Journal of Interpersonal Violence.* 2(1): 82-90.

Bernard, J. L., S. L. Bernard, and M. L. Bernard. 1985. "Courtship Violence and Sex Typing." *Family Relations.* 34:577-581.

Billingham, R. E. 1987. "Courtship Violence: The Patterns of Conflict Resolution Strategies Across Seven Levels of Emotional Commitment." *Family Relations.* 36:283-289.

Burkhart, B. R., and A. L. Staton. 1986. "Sexual Aggression in Acquaintance Relationships." In G. Russel, ed. *Violence in Intimate Relationships*. New York: Spectrum Press.

Carlson, B. E. 1987. "Dating Violence: A Research Review and Comparison with Spouse Abuse." *Social Casework*. 68(1): 16-23.

Cate, R. M., J. M. Henton, J. Koval, F. S. Christopher, and S. Lloyd. 1982. "Pre-Marital Abuse: A Social Psychological Perspective." *Journal of Family Issues*. 3:79-90.

Deal, J. E., and K. S. Wampler. 1986. "Dating Violence: The Primacy of Previous Experience." *Journal of Society and Personality*. 3(4): 457-471.

Flynn, C. P. 1987. "Relationship Violence: A Model for Family Professionals." *Family Relations*. 36:295-299.

Greenblat, C. S. 1983. "A Hit is a Hit is a Hit...or is It? Approval and Tolerance of the Use of Physical Force by Spouses." In D. Finkelhor et al., eds. *The Dark Side of Families*. Beverly Hills, CA: Sage.

Greenblat, C. S. 1985. "Don't Hit Your Wife...Unless: Preliminary Findings on Normative Support for the Use of Physical Force by Husbands." *Victimology*. 10:221-241.

Grusznski, R. J., and T. P. Carrillo. Under review. "Who Completes Batterer's Treatment Groups? An Empirical Investigation." *Journal of Family Violence*.

Lane, K. E., and P. A. Gwartney-Gibbs. 1985. "Violence in the Context of Dating and Sex." *Journal of Family Issues*. 6:45-59.

Laner, M. R. 1983. "Courtship Abuse and Aggression: Contextual Aspects." *Sociological Spectrum*. 3(1): 69-83.

Laner, M. R., and J. Thompson. 1982. "Abuse and Aggression in Courting Couples." *Deviant Behavior*. 3:229-244.

Levine, E. M., and E. J. Kanin. 1987. "Sexual Violence Among Dates and Acquaintances: Trends and Their Implications for Marriage and Family." *Journal of Family Violence*. 2(1): 55-66.

Lloyd, S. A. 1987. "Conflict in Premarital Relationships: Differential Perceptions of Males and Females." *Family Relations*. 36:290-294.

Makepeace, J. M. 1981. "Courtship Violence Among College Students." *Family Relations*. 30:97-102.

Makepeace, J. M. 1983. "Life Events Stress and Courtship Violence." *Family Relations*. 32(1): 101-109.

Makepeace, J. M. 1986. "Gender Differences in Courtship Violence Victimization." *Family Relations*. 35:383-388.

Makepeace, J. M. 1987. "Social Factor and Victim Offender Differences in Courtship Violence." *Family Relations.* 36:87-91.

Matthews, W. J. 1984. "Violence in College Couples." *College Student Journal.* 18:150-158.

O'Keeffe, N. K., K. Brockopp, and E. Chew. 1986. "Teen Dating Violence." *Social Work.* 31(6): 465-471.

Rapaport, K., and R. R. Burkhart. 1984. "Personality and Attitudinal Characteristics of Sexually Coercive College Males." *Journal of Abnormal Psychology.* 93:216-222.

Roark, M. 1987. "Preventing Violence on College Campuses." *Journal of Counseling and Development.* 65(7): 367-372.

Rouse, L. P. 1987. "Abuse in Intimate Relationships: A Comparison of Married and Dating College Students." Paper presented at the Third National Family Violence Research Conference, Durham, NH.

Rust, J. O., and J. Phillips. 1984. "College Students' Perceptions of Spouse Abuse and Conjugal Power." College Student Journal. 18(4): 376-379.

Yllo, K., and M. A. Straus. 1981. "Interpersonal Violence Among Married and Cohabiting Couples." *Family Relations.* 30:339-347.

BATTERED WOMEN

Berk, R. A., P. J. Newton, and S. F. Berk. 1986. "What a Difference a Day Makes: An Empirical Study of the Impact of Shelters for Battered Women." *Journal of Marriage and the Family.* 48:481-490.

Boulette, T. R., and S. M. Andersen. 1985. "'Mind Control' and the Battering of Women." *Community Mental Health Journal.* 21(2): 109-118.

Bowker, L. H., and L. Maurer. 1985. "The Importance of Sheltering in the Lives of Battered Women." *Response.* 8(1): 2-8.

Dutton, D. G., and S. Painter. 1981. "Traumatic Bonding: The Development of Emotional Attachments in Battered Women and Other Relationships of Intermittent Abuse." *Victimology.* 6:139-155.

Dutton, D. G., B. Fehr, and H. McEwen. 1982. "Severe Wife Battering as Deindividuated Violence." *Victimology.* 7:13-23.

Ferraro, K., and J. Johnson. 1983. "How Women Experience Battering." *Social Problems.* 30(3): 325-339.

Frieze, I. H. 1979. "Perceptions of Battered Wives." In I. H. Frieze, D. Bartal, and J. S. Carroll, eds. *New Approaches to Social Problems.* San Francisco: Jossey-Bass.

Gayford, J. 1975. "Battered Wives: A Preliminary Survey of One Hundred Cases." *Medical Science and the Law.* 15:237-245.

Gayford, J. 1977. "The Plight of the Battered Wife." *International Journal of Environmental Studies.* 19(4): 283-286.

Gelles, R. J. 1976. "Abused Women: Why Do They Stay?" *Journal of Marriage and the Family.* 38(3): 659-68.

Gondolf, E. W. Under review. "Battered Women as Survivors: A Causal Model of Helpseeking." *Journal of Marriage & the Family.*

Gondolf, E. W., E. R. Fisher, and J. R. McFerron. In press. "The Helpseeking Behavior of Battered Women: A Preliminary Analysis of Shelter Intake Interviews." *Victimology.*

Goodstein, R., and A. Page. 1981. "Battered Wife Syndrome: Overview of Dynamics and Treatment." *American Journal of Psychiatry.* 138(8): 1036-1043.

Janoff-Bulman, R., and I. Frieze. 1983. "A Theoretical Perspective for Understanding Reactions to Victimization." *Journal of Social Issues.* 39(2): 1-17.

Klein, F. 1983. "Violence Against Women." In B. Haber, ed. *The Women's Annual 1982-1983.* Boston: G. K. Hall.

Lion, J. 1977. "Clinical Aspects of Wifebeating." In M. Roy, ed. *Battered Women.* New York: Van Nostrand Reinhold.

Mills, T. 1985. "The Assault on the Self: Stages in Coping with Battering Husbands." *Qualitative Sociology.* 8(2): 103-123.

Shainess, N. 1977. "Psychological Aspects of Wife Battering." In M. Roy, ed. *Battered Women.* New York: Van Nostrand Reinhold.

Shainess, N. 1979. "Vulnerability to Violence: Masochism as a Process." *American Journal of Psychotherapy.* 33:174-189.

Snell, J., R. Rosenwald, and A. Rokey. 1964. "The Wife Beater's Wife." *Archives of General Psychiatry.* 11:680-684.

Strube, M. J., and L. S. Barboru. 1983. "The Decision to Leave an Abusive Relationship: Economic Dependence and Psychological Commitment." *Journal of Marriage and the Family.* 45(4): 785-793.

U.S. Commission on Civil Rights. 1978. *Battered Women: Issues of Public Policy.* A consultation sponsored by the U.S. Commission on Civil Rights, Washington, DC.

Walker, L. 1983. "The Battered Woman Syndrome Study." In D. Finkelhor et al., eds. *The Dark Side of Families.* Beverly Hills, CA: Sage.

Roots of Wife Battering

— Patriarchy and Relationships —

PATRIARCHY AND FEMINIST THEORY

Bernard, J. 1981. *The Female World.* New York: Free Press.

Brownmiller, S. 1975. *Against Our Will: Men, Women and Rape.* New York: Simon & Schuster.

Chodorow, N. 1978. *The Reproduction of Mothering: Psychoanalysis and the Sociology of Gender.* Berkeley, CA: Univ. of California Press.

Davies, A. 1981. *Women, Race and Class.* New York: Vintage.

Dinnerstein, D. 1976. *The Mermaid and the Minotaur: Sexual Arrangements and the Human Malaise.* New York: Harper & Row.

Donovan, J. 1985. *Feminist Theory: Intellectual Traditions of American Feminism.* New York: Frederick Unger.

Dworkin, A. 1974. *Woman Hating.* New York: E. P. Dutton.

Dworkin, A. 1981. *Pornography: Men Possessing Women.* New York: Perigree Books.

Eisenstein, Z. R. 1984. *Feminism and Sexual Equality.* New York: Monthly Review Press.

Friedan, B. 1981. *The Second Stage.* New York: Summit Books.

Gilligan, C. 1982. *In a Different Voice: Psychological Theory and Women's Development.* Cambridge, MA: Harvard Univ. Press.

Gray, E. D. 1982. *Patriarchy as a Conceptual Trap.* Wellesley, MA: Roundtable Press.

Hooks, B. 1981. *Ain't I A Woman: Black Women and Feminism.* Boston, MA: South End Press.

Hooks, B. 1984. "Feminist Movement to End Violence." In B. Hooks *Feminist Theory: From Margin to Center.* Boston: South End Press.

Jaggar, A., and P. Rothenberg, eds. 1984. *Feminist Frameworks.* New York: McGraw-Hill.

Jardine, A., and P. Smith, eds. 1987. *Men in Feminism.* New York: Methuen.

Morgan, R. 1984. *The Anatomy of Freedom: Feminism, Physics, and Global Politics.* Garden City, NY: Anchor/Doubleday.

Schwendinger, J., and H. Schwendinger. 1983. *Rape and Inequality.* Beverly Hills, CA: Sage.

Singer, J. 1977. *Androgyny: Toward a New Theory of Sexuality.* Garden City, NY: Anchor Books.

Tavris, C., and C. Offir. 1977. *The Longest War: Sex Differences in Perspective.* New York: Harcourt Brace Jovanovich.

Trask, H. K. 1986. *Eros and Power: The Promise of Feminist Theory.* Philadelphia: Univ. of Pennsylvania Press.

Wallace, M. 1979. *Black Macho and the Myth of the Superwoman.* New York: Dial Press.

RELATIONSHIP ISSUES

Atkinson, J. 1987 "Gender Roles in Marriage and the Family: A Critique and Some Proposals." *Journal of Family Issues.* 8(1): 5-41.

Ashmore, R. D., and F. K. Del Boca. 1986. *The Social Psychology of Male-Female Relations: A Critical Analysis of Central Concepts.* Orlando, FL: Academic Press.

Berk, S. F. 1985. *The Gender Factory: The Apportionment of Work in American Households.* New York: Plenum Press.

Blumstein, P., and P. Schwartz. 1983. *American Couples.* New York: William Morrow.

Burger, A. L., and N. S. Jacobson. 1979. "The Relationship Between Sex Role Characteristics in Couple Satisfaction and Couple Problem-Solving Skills." *American Journal of Family Therapy.* 7:5-10.

Cromwell, R., and D. Olson, eds. 1975. *Power in Families.* New York: Wiley.

Franklin, C. W. 1980. "White Racism as a Cause of Black Male-Black Female Conflict." *Western Journal of Black Studies.* 4:42-48.

Goldberg, H. 1983. *The New Male-Female Relationship.* New York: Signet Books.

Kimball, G. 1983. *The 50-50 Marriage.* Boston: Beacon Press.

Kramerae, C. 1981. *Women and Men Speaking.* Rowley, MA: Newberry House.

Kranichfeld, M. L. 1987. "Rethinking Family Power." *Journal of Family Issues.* 8(1): 42-56.

Krausz, S. L. 1986. "Sex Roles within Marriage." *Social Work.* 31:457-464.

Kyle, S. O., and T. Falbo. 1985. "Relationships Between Marital Stress and Attributional Preferences for Own and Spouse Behavior." *Journal of Social and Clinical Psychology.* 3(3): 339-351.

Laing, R. D. 1969. *The Politics of the Family and Other Essays.* New York: Vintage.

Luria, Z., S. Friedman, and M. D. Rose. 1986. *Human Sexuality.* New York: Wiley.

Mirowsky, J. 1985. "Depression and Marital Power: An Equity Model." *American Journal of Sociology.* 91(3): 557-592.

Pitcher, E. and L. S. Schultz. 1983. *Boys and Girls At Play: The Development of Sex Roles.* New York: Praeger.

Pleck, J. 1985. *Working Wives, Working Husbands.* Beverly Hills, CA: Sage.

Rich, A. 1979. *On Lies, Secrets, and Silence.* New York: W.W. Norton.

Rubin, L. 1976. *Worlds of Pain: Life in the Working Class Family.* New York: Basic.

Rubin, L. 1983. *Intimate Strangers: Men and Women Together.* New York: Harper & Row.

Sanford, J. 1980. *The Invisible Partners: How The Male and Female in Each of Us Affects Our Relationships.* New York: Paulist Press.

Stockard, J., and M. M. Journson. 1980. *Sex Roles: Sex Inequality and Sex Role Development.* Englewood Cliffs, NJ: Prentice-Hall.

Scanzoni, J. 1978. *Sex Roles, Women's Work, and Marital Conflict.* Lexington, MA: Lexington.

Scanzoni, J. 1982 (1972). *Sexual Bargaining: Power and Politics in the American Marriage.* 2d ed. Chicago: Univ. of Chicago Press.

Warner, R. L., G. R. Lee, and J. Lee. 1986. "Social Organization, Spousal Resources, and Marital Power: A Cross-Cultural Study." *Journal of Marriage and the Family.* 48:121-128.

Weis, D. L., and J. R. Felton. 1987. "Marital Exlusivity and the Potential for Future Marital Conflict." *Social Work.* 32(1): 45-49.

— Masculinity and Sex-Roles —

MASCULINITY BOOKS

The Nature of Masculinity

Abbott, F., ed. 1987. *New Men, New Minds: Breaking Male Tradition.* Freedom, CA: Crossing Press.

Bell, D. 1982. *Being a Man: The Paradox of Masculinity*. Brattleboro, VT: Greene.

Blos, P. 1985. *Sons and Fathers: Before and Beyond the Oedipus Complex*. New York: Free Press.

Blumenthal, M., R. Kahn, F. Andrews, and K. Head. 1972. *Justifying Violence: Attitudes and American Men*. Ann Arbor, MI: Institute for Social Research, Univ. of Michigan.

Brod, H., ed. 1987. *The Making of Masculinities: The New Men's Studies*. Winchester, MA: Allen & Unwin.

Brothers, J. 1981. *What Every Woman Should Know About Men*. New York: Simon & Schuster.

Cottle, T. J. 1981. *Like Father, Like Son: Portraits of Intimacy and Strain*. Norwood, NJ: Ablex.

Fini, R. 1987. *Forgotten Man: Understanding the Male Psyche*. New York: Harrington Park Press.

Friedman, R., and L. Lerner, eds. 1987. *Toward a New Psychology of Men: Psychoanalytic and Social Perspectives*. New York: Guilford.

Gary, L. E. 1981. *Black Men*. Beverly Hills, CA: Sage.

Gordon, J. 1982. *The Myth of the Monstrous Male*. New York: Playboy.

Hapgood, Fred. 1979. *Why Males Exist*. New York: William Morrow.

Hess, B. B., and M. M. Feree. 1987. *Analyzing Gender: A Handbook of Social Science Research*. Beverly Hills, CA: Sage.

Hite, S. 1981. *The Hite Report on Male Sexuality*. New York: Knopf.

Johnson, R. 1977. *He: Understanding Masculine Psychology*. New York: Perennial Library.

Komarovsky, M. 1975. *Dilemmas of Masculinity: A Study of College Youth*. New York: Norton.

Lein, L., and M. B. Sussman, eds. 1983. *The Ties That Bind: Men's and Women's Social Networks*. New York: Haworth Press.

Levinson, D. 1978. *The Seasons of a Man's Life*. New York: Knopf.

Lewis, R., ed. 1981. *Men In Difficult Times*. Englewood Cliffs, NJ: Prentice-Hall.

Miller, S. 1983. *Men and Friendship*. Boston: Houghton Mifflin.

Pleck, J. H. 1981. *The Myth of Masculinity*. Cambridge: MIT Press.

Shanor, Karen. 1978. *The Shanor Study: The Sexual Sensitivity of the American Male*. New York: Dial Press.

Shostak, A. B., and G. McLouth. 1984. *Men and Abortion: Lessons, Losses, and Love*. New York: Praeger.

Stearns, P. 1979. *Be A Man: Males in Modern Society*. New York: Holmes & Meier.

Tiger, L. 1970. *Men in Groups*. New York: Vintage.

Vaillant, G. E. 1977. *Adaptation to Life*. Boston: Little, Brown.

Zilbergeld, B. 1978. *Male Sexuality: A Guide to Self-Fulfillment*. Boston: Little, Brown.

Problems of Masculinity

Chesler, P. 1978. *About Men*. New York: Simon & Schuster.

DeCecco, J. 1984. *Bashers, Baiters and Bigots: Homophobia in American Society*. New York: Harrington Park Press.

Derber, C. 1983. *The Pursuit of Attention: Power and Individualism in Everyday Personality Life*. New York: Oxford Univ. Press.

Ehrenreich, B. 1983. *The Hearts of Men: American Dreams and the Flight from Commitment*. New York: Doubleday.

Etheredge, L. 1978. *A World of Men: Masculinity in U.S. Foreign Policy*. Cambridge, MA: MIT Press.

Fasteau, M. 1974. *The Male Machine*. New York: McGraw-Hill.

Goldberg, H. 1976. *The Hazards of Being Male*. New York: Nash.

Holliday, L. 1978. *The Violent Sex: Male Psychobiology and the Evolution of Consciousness*. Guerneville, CA: Bluestocking Books.

Jamus, S., B. Bess, and C. Saltus. 1977. *A Sexual Profile of Men in Power*. New York: Warner Books.

Kiley, D. 1983. *The Peter Pan Principle: Men Who Have Never Grown Up*. New York: Dodd Mead.

Kohn, A. 1986. *No Contest: The Case Against Competition*. New York: Houghton Mifflin.

McClelland, D. 1976. *Power: The Inner Experience*. New York: Halsted Press.

Naifeh, S., and G. W. Smith. 1984. *Why Can't Men Open Up?* New York: Clarkson N. Potter.

Osherson, S. 1980. *Holding On or Letting: Men and Career Change at Midlife*. New York: Free Press.

Ryan, F. 1981. *Sports and Psychology*. Englewood Cliffs, NJ: Prentice-Hall.

Sexton, P. 1973. *The Feminized Male: Classrooms, White Collar, and the Decline of Manliness*. New York: Vintage.

Toch, H. 1969. *Violent Men: An Inquiry into the Psychology of Violence*. Hawthorne, NY: Aldine.

Wilkinson, R. 1986. *American Tough: The Tough-Guy Tradition and American Character*. New York: Harper & Row.

Wrong, D. 1979. *Power: Its Forms, Bases, and Uses.* New York: Harper & Row.

Changing Men

Arcana, J. 1983. *Every Mother's Son: The Role of Mother's in the Making of Men.* Garden City, NY: Doubleday.

Astrachan, A. 1986. *How Men Feel: Their Response to Women's Demands for Equality and Power.* Garden City, NY: Anchor/ Doubleday.

Baumli, F., ed. 1985. *Men Freeing Men: An Anthology of Writings on Men's Liberation.* Jersey City, NJ: New Atlantis Press.

David, D., and R. Brannon, eds. 1982. *The Forty-Nine Percent Majority: The Male Sex Role.* 2d ed. Reading, MA: Addison-Wesley.

Diamond, J. 1983. *Inside Out: Becoming My Own Man.* San Rafael, CA: Fifth Wave Press.

Dittes, J. 1985. *The Male Predicament: On Being A Man Today.* New York: Harper & Row.

Doyle, J. A. 1983. *The Male Experience.* Dubuque, IA: William C. Brown.

Druck, K., with J. Simmons. 1985. *Secrets Men Keep.* New York: Doubleday.

Ellis, A. 1976. *Sex and the Liberated Man.* Secaucus, NJ: Lyle Stuart.

Farrell, W. 1975. *The Liberated Man.* New York: Bantam.

Farrell, W. 1986. *Why Men Are The Way They Are.* New York: McGraw-Hill.

Friedman, R. M., and L. Lerner, eds. 1987. *Toward a New Psychology of Men: Psychoanalytic and Social Perspectives.* New York: Guilford.

Garfinkel, P. 1985. *In a Man's World: Father, Son, Brother, Friend and Other Roles Men Play.* New York, NY: New Amer. Library.

Gerzon, M. 1982. *A Choice of Heroes: The Changing Faces of Manhood.* New York: Houghton Mifflin.

Goldberg, H. 1979. *The New Male: From Self-Destruction to Self Care.* New York: William Morrow.

Kimmel, M. S., ed. 1987. *Changing Men: New Directions in Research on Men and Masculinity.* Beverly Hills, CA: Sage.

Lewis, C., and M. O'Brien, eds. 1987. *Reassessing Fatherhood.* Beverly Hills, CA: Sage.

Lewis, R., and M. Sussman, eds. 1986. *Men's Changing Roles in the Family.* New York: Haworth Press.

Lyon, H. 1978. *Tenderness Is Strength: From Machismo to Manhood.* New York: Harper & Row.

Nichols, J. 1974. *Men's Liberation: A New Definition of Masculinity.* New York: Penguin.

Osherson, S. 1986. *Finding Our Fathers: The Unfinished Business of Manhood.* New York: Free Press.

Pleck, J., and J. Sawyer, eds. 1974. *Men and Masculinity.* New York: Prentice-Hall.

Pruett, K. D. 1987. *The Nurturing Father.* New York: Warner Books.

Schenk, R. U. 1982. *The Other Side of the Coin: Causes and Consequences of Men's Oppression.* Madison, WI: Bioenergetics Press.

Scher, M., M. Stevens, G. Good, and G. Eichenfield, eds. 1987. *Handbook of Counseling and Psychotherapy with Men.* Beverley Hills, CA: Sage.

Shapiro, E., and B. Shapiro, eds. 1979. *The Women Say/The Men Say: The Women's Liberation Movement and Men's Consciousness.* New York: Dell.

Snodgrass, J, ed. 1977. *For Men Against Sexism.* New York: Times Change Press.

Solomon, K., and N. Levy, eds. 1982. *Men in Transition: Theory and Therapy.* New York: Plenum Press.

Tolson, A. 1977. *The Limits of Masculinity: Male Identity and Women's Liberation.* New York: Harper & Row.

MASCULINITY PAPERS

The Nature of Masculinity

Fein, R. 1977. "Examining the Nature of Masculinity." In S. Sargent, ed. *Beyond Sex Roles.* St. Paul, MN: West Pub.

Fein, R. A. 1978. "Research in Fathering: Social Policy and an Emergent Perspective." *Journal of Social Issues.* 34:122-135.

Hare, N. 1971. "The Frustrated Masculinity of the Negro Male." In R. Staples, ed. *The Black Family.* Belmont, CA: Wadsworth.

Hooberman, R. E. 1979. "Psychological Androgyny, Feminine Gender Identity and Self-Esteem in Homosexual and Heterosexual Males." *Journal of Sex Research.* 15:306-315.

Lewis, R. A. 1978. "Emotional Intimacy Among Men." *Journal of Social Issues.* 34:109-121.

Osherson, S., and D. Dill. 1983. "Varying Work and Family Choices: Their Impact on Men's Work Satisfaction." *Journal of Marriage and the Family*. 43:339-346.

Pleck, J. H. 1976. "The Male Sex Role: Definitions, Problems, and Sources of Change." *Journal of Social Issues*. 32:155-164.

Pleck, J. H. 1979. "Men's Family Work: Three Perspectives and Some New Data." *Family Coordinator*. 24(4): 481-488.

Polatnick, M. 1973. "Why Men Don't Rear Children: A Power of Analysis." *Berkeley Journal of Sociology*. 45-86.

Shively, M. G. and J. P. De Cecco. 1977. "Components of Sexual Identity." *Journal of Homosexuality*. 3:41-48.

Skovholt, T. 1978. "Feminism and Men's Lives." *Counseling Psychologist*. 7(4): 3-10.

Staples, R. 1978. "Masculinity and Race: The Dual Dilemma of Black Men." *Journal of Social Issues*. 34:169-183.

Thompson, K. 1982. "What Men Really Want: An Interview with Robert Bly." *New Age*. May:50.

Wise, S., and L. Stanley. 1984 "Men and Sex: A Case Study in 'Sexual Politics'" (Special Issue). *Women's Studies International Forum*. 7:1.

Zimmerman, D. H., and C. West. 1975. "Sex Roles, Interruptions, and Silences in Conversation." In B. Thorne and N. Henley, eds. *Language and Sex: Difference and Dominance*. Rowley, MA: Newberry House.

Male Socialization

Burnett, E. C., and J. Daniels. 1985. "The Impact of Family of Origin and Stress on Interpersonal Conflict Resolution Skills in Young Adult Men." *American Mental Health Counsel Association Journal*. 7(4): 162-171.

Cohen, T. F. 1987. "Remaking Men: Men's Experiences Becoming and Being Husbands and Fathers and Their Implications for Reconceptualizing Men's Lives." *Journal of Family Issues*. 8(1): 57-77.

Crosby, F., and G. M. Herek. 1986. "Male Sympathy with the Situation of Women: Does Personal Experience Make a Difference?" *Journal of Social Issues*. 42(2): 55-67.

Hartley, R. 1974. "Sex Role Pressures and the Socialization of the Male Child." In J. Pleck and J. Sawyer, eds. *Men and the Masculinity*. Englewood Cliffs, NJ: Prentice-Hall.

Henslin, J. 1981. "On Becoming Male: Reflections of a Sociologist on Childhood and Early Socialization." In J. Henslin, ed. *Down to Earth Sociology.* 3d ed. New York: Free Press.

McBroom, W. H. 1981. "Parental Relationships and Socioeconomic Status and Sex-Role Expectations." *Sex Roles.* 7:1027-1034.

Thorton, A., D. F. Alwin, and D. Camburn. 1983. "Causes and Consequences of Sex-Role Attitudes and Attitude Change." *American Sociology Review.* 48:221-227.

Toomey, K. 1977. "Johnny, I Hardly Knew Ye: Toward a Revision of the Theory of Male Psychosexual Development." *American Journal of Orthopsychiatry.* 47:184-95.

The Male Sex-Role

Balswick, J. O. 1979. "The Inexpressive Male: Functional-Conflict and Role Theory as Contrasting Explanations." *Family Coordinator.* 28(3): 331-335.

Balswick, J.O., and C. W. Peck. 1971."The Inexpressive Male: A Tragedy of American Society." *The Family Coordinator.* 20:363-368.

Biaggio, M.K., and A. Brownell. 1986. "Gender Differences in Anger Expression: The Paradox of Victim Blame." Paper presented at the Women in Psychology Association, Seattle, WA.

Goode, W. J. 1982. "Why Men Resist." In B. Thorne and M. Yalom, eds. *Rethinking the Family.* New York: Longmans.

Harrison, J. 1978. "Warning: The Male Sex Role May Be Hazardous to Your Health." *Journal of Social Issues.* 34:65-86.

Horney, K. 1932. "The Dread of Women." *International Journal of Psychoanalysis.* 13:138.

Hoschchild, A. R. 1975. "The Sociology of Feeling and Emotion: Selected Possibilities." In M. Millman and R. M. Kanter, eds. *Another Voice: Feminist Perspectives on Social Life and Social Science.* Garden City, NY: Anchor/Doubleday.

Lehne, G. K. 1976. "Homophobia Among Men." In D. David and R. Brannon, eds. *The Forty-Nine Percent Majority.* Reading, MA: Addison-Wesley.

Meinecke, C. 1981. "Socialized to Die Younger? Hypermasculinity and Men's Health." *Personnel and Guidance Journal.* 60(4): 241-245.

Morin, S. F. 1974. "Educational Programs as a Means of Changing Attitudes Toward Gay People." *Homosexual Counseling Journal.* 1(4): 160-165.

Morin, S. F., and E. M. Garfinkel. 1978. "Male Homophobia." *Journal of Social Issues.* 34(1): 29-48.

Marolla, J., and D. Scully. 1986. "Attitudes Toward Women, Violence, and Rape: A Comparison of Convicted Rapists and Other Felons." *Deviant Behavior.* 7(4): 337-355.

O'Neal, J. M. 1981. "Patterns of Gender Role Conflict and Strain: Sexism and Fear of Femininity in Men's Lives." *Personnel and Guidance Journal.* 60(4): 203-210.

O'Neal, J. M. 1982. "Gender Role Conflict and Strain in Men's Lives." In K. Solomon and N. Levy, eds. *Men in Transition.* New York: Plenum Press.

Pleck, J. H. 1976. "Male Threat From Female Competence." *Journal of Consulting & Clinical Psychology.* 44:608-613.

Sattel, J. W. 1976. "The Inexpressive Male: Tragedy or Sexual Politics." *Social Problems.* 28:469-477.

Sattel, J. W. 1983. "Men, Inexpressiveness, and Power." In B. Thorne, C. Kramarae, and N. Henley, eds. *Language, Gender and Society.* Rowley, MA: Newberry House.

Scher, M. 1981. "Men in Hiding: A Challenge for the Counselor." *Personnel and Guidance Journal.* 60(4): 199-203.

Control and Oppression

Crites, J., and L. Fitzgerald. 1978. "The Competent Male." *The Counseling Psychologist.* 7(4): 10-14.

DeVoe, M. W. 1977. "Cooperation as a Function of Self-Concept, Sex and Race." *Educational Research Quarterly.* 2:3-8.

Farrell, M. 1986. "Friendship Between Men." In R. Lewis and M. Sussman, eds. *Men's Changing Roles in the Family.* New York: Haworth Press.

Klein, M. 1985. "Time for Men's Liberation." *Women and Therapy.* 42:23-28.

Komisar, L. 1976. "Violence and the Masculine Mystique." In D. David and R. Brannon, eds. *The Forty-Nine Percent Majority: The Male Sex Role.* Reading, MA: Addison-Wesley.

Litewka, J. 1979. "The Socialized Penis." In E. Shapiro and B. Shapiro, eds. *The Women Say/The Men Say: The Women's Liberation Movement and Men's Consciousness.* New York: Dell.

Malamuth, N. 1981. "Rape Proclivity Among Males." *Journal of Social Issues.* 37:138-154.

Marciano, T. D. 1986. "Why are Men Unhappy in Patriarchy?" In R. Lewis and M. Sussman, eds. *Men's Changing Roles in the Family.* New York: Haworth Press.

O'Neal, J. 1981. "Patterns of Gender Role Conflict and Strain: Sexism and Fear of Femininity in Men's Lives." *Personnel and Guidance Journal.* 60(4): 203-210.

Pleck, J. H. 1979. "Men's Power with Women, Other Men and Society: A Men's Movement Analysis. In E. Shapiro and B. Shapiro, eds. *The Women Say/The Men Say: Women's Liberation and Men's Consciousness.* New York: Dell.

Schoenbach, C. 1985. "Effects of Husband's and Wife's Social Status on Psychological Functioning." *Journal of Marriage and the Family.* 47(3): 597-607.

Shepard, H. 1977. "Men in Organizations: Some Reflections." In S. Sargent, ed. *Beyond Sex Roles.* St. Paul, MN: West Pub.

Stodder, J. 1979. "Confessions of a Candy-Ass Roughneck." In E. Shapiro and B. Shapiro, eds. *The Women Say/The Men Say: Women's Liberation and Men's Consciousness.* New York: Dell.

Stone, I. F. 1974. "Machismo in Washington." In J. H. Pleck and J. Sawyer, eds. *Men and Masculinity.* Englewood Cliffs, NJ: Prentice-Hall.

— Anger, Aggression and Violence —

ANGER

Averill, J. 1984. *Anger and Aggression: An Essay on Emotion.* New York: Springer-Verlag.

Berkowitz, L. 1983. "The Experience of Anger as a Parallel Process." In R. G. Geen and E. I. Donnerstein, eds. *Aggression: Theoretical and Empirical Reviews,* Volume 1. New York: Academic Press.

Gaylin, W. 1984. *The Rage Within: Anger in Modern Life.* New York: Simon & Schuster.

Stearns, C. Z., and P. Stearns. 1986. *Anger: The Struggle for Emotional Control in America's History.* Chicago: Univ. of Chicago Press.

Tavris, C. 1982. *Anger: The Misunderstood Emotion.* New York: Simon & Schuster.

AGGRESSION

Bandura, A. 1983. "Psychological Mechanisms of Aggression." In R. G. Geen and E. I. Donnerstein, eds. *Aggression: Theoretical and Empirical Reviews,* Volume 2. New York: Academic Press.

Berkowitz, L. 1962. *Aggression: A Social Psychological Analysis.* New York: McGraw-Hill.

Berkowitz, L. 1983. "The Goals of Aggression." In D. Finkelhor et al., eds. *The Dark Side of Families.* Beverly Hills, CA: Sage.

Blanchard, R. J., and D. C. Blanchard, eds. 1986. *Advances in the Study of Aggression.* Orlando, FL: Academic Press.

Dollard, J., N. E. Miller, L. W. Doob, O.H. Mowrer, and R. R. Sears. 1939. *Frustration and Aggression.* New Haven: Yale Univ. Press.

Geen, R. G., and E. C. O'Neal, eds. 1976. *Perspective on Aggression.* New York: Academic Press.

Geen , R. G., and E. I. Donnerstein, eds. 1983. *Aggression: Theoretical and Empirical Reviews,* Volume 2. New York: Academic Press.

Gerard, N. 1987. *Origins of Human Aggression: Dynamics and Etiology.* New York: Human Sciences Press.

Goldstein, A., ed. 1981. *In Response to Aggression: Methods of Control and Prosocial Alternatives.* New York: Pergamon.

Hills, S. L. 1980. *Demystifying Social Deviance.* New York: McGraw-Hill.

Letourneau, C. 1981. "Empathy and Stress: How They Affect Parental Aggression." *Social Work.* 26:307-316.

Lorenz, K. 1977. *On Aggression.* New York: Bantam.

Malamuth, N. M., and E. I. Donnerstein, eds. 1984. *Pornography and Sexual Aggression.* Orlando, FL: Academic Press.

Montagu, A. 1973. *Man and Aggression.* 2d ed. New York: Oxford Univ. Press.

Moyer, K. E. 1976. *The Psychology of Aggression.* New York: Harper & Row.

Neuman, G., ed. 1987. *Origins of Human Aggression: Dynamics and Etiology.* New York: Human Sciences Press.

Ponton, E. 1986. "Some Issues Concerning Aggression and Violence in Human Beings." *Psychology.* 23(2-3): 30-34.

Williams, T. M., M. L. Zabrack, and L. A. Joy. 1982. "The Portrayal of Aggression on North American T.V." *Journal of Applied Social Psychology.* 12(5): 360-380.

VIOLENCE

Ball-Rokeach, S. J. 1980. "Normative and Deviant Violence from a Conflict Perspective." *Social Problems.* 28:45-62.

Berkowitz, L. 1979. "Is Criminal Violence Normative Behavior: Hostile and Instrumental Aggression in Violent Incidents." *Journal of Research of Crime and Delinquency.* July:148-161.

Campbell, A., and J. Gibbs, eds. 1986. *Violent Transactions: The Limits of Personality.* New York: Basil Blackwell.

Curtis, G. C. 1963. "Violence Breeds Violence -- Perhaps?" *American Journal of Psychiatry.* 120:376-387.

Fromm, E. 1973. *The Anatomy of Human Destructiveness.* New York: Random House.

Gilula, M. F., and D. N. Daniels. 1969. "Violence and Man's Struggle to Adapt." *Science.* 64:396-405.

Goldstein, J. 1986. *Aggression and Crimes of Violence.* 2d ed. New York: Oxford Univ. Press.

Haynie, R. L. 1980. "Deprivation of Body Pleasure: Origins of Violent Behavior (A Survey of the Literature)." *Child Welfare.* 5:277-297.

Huesmann, L. R., and N. M. Malamuth. 1986. "Media Violence and Antisocial Behavior: An Overview." *Journal of Social Issues.* 42(3): 1-7.

Lefkowitz, M. M., L. D., Eron, L. O. Walder, and L. R. Hussman. 1977. *Growing Up to Be Violent.* Hinsdale, IL: Dryden.

May, R. 1972. *Power and Innocence: A Search for the Sources of Violence.* New York: Norton.

Monahan, J. 1981. *Predicting Violent Behavior: An Assessment of Clinical Techniques.* Beverly Hills, CA: Sage.

Moyer, K. E. 1987. *Violence and Aggression: A Psychological Perspective.* New York: Paragon House.

Newman, G. 1979. *Understanding Violence.* New York: J. B. Lippincott.

Prescott, J. 1975. "Body Pleasure and the Origins of Violence." *Bulletin of the Atomic Scientists.* November:10-20.

Riches, D., ed. 1987. *The Anthropology of Violence.* New York: Basil Blackwell.

Saunders, S. et al., eds. 1984. *Violent Individuals and Families: A Handbook for Practitioners.* Springfield, IL: C. C. Thomas.

Stewart, R. B., ed. 1981. *Violent Behavior: Social Learning Approaches to Prediction, Management, and Treatment.* New York: Brunner/ Mazel.

Men Who Batter

— Batterer Characteristics —

COUPLES COMPARISONS

Bograd, M. 1983. "Domestic Violence: Perceptions of Battered Women, Abusive Men, and Non-Violent Men and Woman." Ph.D. diss. University of Chicago.

Carlson, B. 1977. "Battered Women and Their Assailants." *Social Work.* 22(6): 455-465.

Gray, L. 1987. "Predicting Interpersonal Conflict Between Men and Women." In M. S. Kimmel, ed. 1987. *Changing Men: New Directions in Research on Men and Masculinity.* Beverly Hills, CA: Sage.

Kleckner, J. 1978. "Wife Beaters and Beaten Wives: Co-Conspirators in Crimes of Violence." *Psychology.* 15:54-56.

Rosenbaum, A., and K. D. O'Leary. 1981. "Marital Violence: Characteristics of Abusive Couples." *Journal of Consulting & Clinical Psychology.* 49:63-71.

Roy, M. 1977. "Current Survey of 150 Cases." In M. Roy, ed. *Battered Women.* New York: Van Nostrand Reinhold.

Roy, M. 1982. "Four Thousands Partners in Violence: A Trend Analysis." In M. Roy, ed. *The Abusive Partner.* New York: Van Nostrand Reinhold.

Shields, N. M., and C. R. Hanneke. 1983. "Attribution Processes in Violent Relationships: Perceptions of Violent Husbands and Their Wives." *Journal of Applied Social Psychology.* 13(6): 515-527.

Steinmetz, S. 1980. "Women and Violence: Victims and Perpetrators." *American Journal of Psychotherapy.* 34:334-349.

Straus, M. A. 1980. "Victims and Aggressors in Marital Violence." *American Behavioral Scientist.* 23:681-704.

Telch, C. F., and C. U. Lindquist. 1984. "Violent Versus Non-Violent Couples: A Comparisons of Patterns." *Psychotherapy.* 21:242-248.

SEX-ROLE AND SELF-ESTEEM

Barnett, O. W., and A. R. Lindsay, 1985. "Therapists' Evaluations of Batterers' Stresses, Moods, and Power Relations." Paper presented at Women in Psychology Association, San Jose, CA.

Barnett, O. W., and T. A. Ryska. 1986. "Masculinity and Femininity in Maritally Violent Males." Paper presented at the American Society of Criminology, Atlanta, GA.

Fitch, F., and A. Papantonio. 1983. "Men Who Batter: Some Pertinent Characteristics." *Journal of Nervous and Mental Disease.* 171(3): 190-192.

Friedman, D. H. 1982. *"Locus of Control, Self-Esteem, and Dogmatism in Male Marine Spouse Abusers."* Master's thesis, University of Washington, Seattle.

Goldstein, D., and A. Rosenbaum. 1985. "An Evaluation of the Self-Esteem of Maritally Violent Men." *Family Relations.* 34:425-428.

LaViolette, A. D., O. W. Barnett. and C. L. Miller. 1984. "A Classification of Wife on the Bem Sex-Role Inventory." Paper presented at the Second National Conference for Family Violence Researchers, Durham, NH.

Long, V. O. 1986. "Relationship of Masculinity to Self-Esteem and Self-Acceptance in Female Professionals, College Students, Clients, and Victims of Domestic Violence." *Journal of Consulting & Clinical Psychology.* 54(3): 323-327.

Lopez, S. C. 1981. "Marital Satisfaction and Wife Abuse as a Function of Sex-Role Identity, Self-Esteem, and Interpersonal Style." Ph.D. diss., Georgia State University.

Neidig, P. N., D. H. Friedman, and B. S. Collins. 1986. "Attitudinal Characteristics of Males Who Have Engaged in Spouse Abuse." *Journal of Family Violence.* 1(3): 223-234.

Rosenbaum, A. 1986. "Of Men, Macho, and Marital Violence." *Journal of Family Violence.* 1(2): 121-130.

Rouse, L. P. 1984. "Models, Self-Esteem, and Locus of Control as Factors Contributing to Spouse Abuse." *Victimology.* 9(1): 130-144.

PERSONALITY TRAITS

Bolton, F. G., and S. R. Bolton. 1987. "The Perpetrator in the Violent Family." In F. G. Bolton and S. R. Bolton. *Victimization Within Families.* Beverly Hills: Sage.

Browning, J. J. 1984. "Violence Against Intimates: Toward a Profile of the Wife Assaulter." Ph.D. diss,. University of British Columbia.

Ceasar, P. L. 1986. "Men Who Batter: A Heterogeneous Group." Paper presented at American Psychological Association, Wash., DC.

Coleman, K. H. 1980. "Conjugal Violence: What 33 Men Report." *Journal of Marriage and Family Counseling.* April:207-213.

Elbow, M. 1977. "Theoretical Considerations of Violent Marriages (Personality characteristics of wife abusers)." *Social Casework.* 58:515-526.

Faulk, M. 1974. "Men Who Assault Their Wives." *Medicine, Science, and Law.* 14:180-183.

Gondolf, E. W. Forthcoming. "Who Are Those Guys? A Behavioral Typology of Men Who Batter Based on Shelter Interviews." *Violence and Victims.*

Grusznski, R. J., and T. P. Carrillo. Under review. "Who Completes Batterer's Treatment Groups? An Empirical Investigation." *Journal of Family Violence.*

Hamberger, K. L., and J. E. Hastings. 1986. "Personality Correlates of Men Who Abuse Their Partners: A Cross-Validation Study." *Journal of Family Violence.* 1(4): 323-331.

Hoshmand, L. T. Forthcoming. "Client's and Therapist's Judgement of Anger Problems in Batterers and Nonbatterers." *Journal of Interpersonal Violence.*

Kuhl, A. F. 1981. "A Preliminary Profile of Abusing Men." Paper presented at Academy for Criminal Justice Sciences, Philadelphia.

Maiuro, R. D., T. S. Cahn, and P. P. Vitaliano. 1986. "Assertiveness Deficits and Hostility in Domestically Violent Men." *Violence and Victims.* 1(4): 279-290.

Mederos, F. R. 1987. "Men Who Abuse Women and 'Normal' Men: Theorizing Continuities and Discontinuities." Paper presented at Third National Family Violence Research Conference, Durham, NH.

Ponzetti, J. J., R. M. Cate, and J. E. Koval. 1982. "Violence Between Couples: Profiling the Male Abuser." *Personnel and Guidance Journal.* 61(4): 220-224.

Roy, M., ed. 1982. *The Abusive Partner.* New York: Van Nostrand Reinhold.

Ryan, D. M. 1981. "Patterns of Antecedents to Husbands' Battering Behavior as Detected by the Use of the Critical Incident Technique." Ph.D. diss., United States International University.

Saunders, D. G. 1987. "Are There Different Types of Men Who Batter? An Empirical Study with Possible Treatment Implications." Paper presented at the Third National Family Violence Research Conference, Durham, NH.

Schultz, L. G. 1960. "The Wife Assaulter." *Corrective Psychiatry and Journal of Social Therapy.* 6:103-111.

Shields, N., and C. Hanneke. 1983. "Violent Husbands: Patterns of Individual Violence." Unpublished paper. Policy Research & Planning Group, St. Louis, MO.

Watson, C., A. Rosenberg, and N. Petrik. 1982. "Incidence of Wife-Battering in Male Psychiatric Hospital Patients: Are Special Treatment Programs Needed?" *Psychological Reports.* 51(2): 563-566.

OTHER CHARACTERISTICS

Barnett, O. W., K. E. Butler, and T. A. Ryska. 1987. "Abuse of Batterers and Their Exposure to Violence During Childhood: A Preliminary Report." Paper presented at the Third National Family Violence Research Conference, Durham, NH.

Coates, C. J., and D. J. Leong. 1987. "Personality Differences Among Batterers Voluntarily Seeking Treatment and Those Ordered to Treatment by the Court." Paper presented at the Third National Family Violence Research Conference, Durham, NH.

Cohn, E. G., L. W. Sherman, J. Schmidt, and R. Grimwood. 1987. "Interviews with Arrested Offenders in Milwaukee." Paper presented at the Third National Family Violence Research Conference, Durham, NH.

Edleson, J., I. Eisikovits, and E. Guttman. 1985. "Men Who Batter Women: A Critical Review of the Evidence." *Journal of Family Issues.* 6(2): 229-247.

Eisikovits, Z. C. 1987. "Israeli Men Who Batter: An Ecological Analysis." Paper presented at the Third National Family Violence Research Conference, Durham, NH.

Fagan, J., and S. Wexler. 1987. "Crime at Home and in the Streets: The Relationship between Family and Stranger Violence." *Victims and Violence.* 2(1): 5-24.

Fagan, J., D. Stewart, and K. Hansen. 1983. "Violent Men or Violent Husbands? Background Factors and Situational Correlates." In D. Finkelhor et al., eds. *The Dark Side of Families.* Beverly Hills, CA: Sage.

Gondolf, E. W. 1985. "Anger and Oppression in Men Who Batter: Empiricist and Feminist Perspectives and Their Implications for Research." *Victimology.* 10(1-4): 311-324.

Harris, R. N., and R. W. Bologh. 1985. "The Dark Side of Love: Blue and White Collar Wife Abuse." *Victimology.* 10(1-4): 242-252.

Lohr, J. M., L. K. Hamberger, and J. E. Hastings. 1986. "Cluster Analysis of Personality Disorder in Spouse Abusers." Paper presented at American Psychological Association, Washington, DC.

Ptacek, J. 1987. "Why Do Men Batter Their Wives?" In K. Yllo and M. Bograd, eds. *Feminist Perspectives on Wife Abuse.* Beverly Hills, CA: Sage.

Roberts, A. R. 1987. "Psychosocial Characteristics of Batterers: A Study of 234 Men Charged with Domestic Violence Offenses." *Journal of Family Violence.* 2(1): 81-94.

Safran, C. 1986. "Why Men Hurt the Women They Love." *Reader's Digest.* January:77-81.

Taubman, S. 1986. "Beyond the Bravado: Sex Roles and the Exploitive Male." *Social Work.* 31(1): 12-18.

TREATMENT RESPONSE AND CHANGE

Adams, D. 1984. "Stages of Anti-Sexist Awareness and Change for Men Who Batter." Paper presented at the American Psychological Association, Toronto, Canada.

Adams, D., and I. Penn. 1981. "Men in Groups: The Socialization of Men Who Batter." Paper presented at the American Orthopsychiatric Association, New York, NY.

Bern, E. H. 1982. "From Violent Incident to Spouse Abuse Syndrome." *Social Casework.* 63:41-45.

Bernard, J. L., and M. L. Bernard. 1984. "The Abusive Male Seeking Treatment: Jekyll and Hyde." *Family Relations.* 33:543-547.

Dutton, D. G. 1984. "A Psychological Nested Theory of Male Violence Towards Intimates." In P. Caplan, ed. *Feminist Psychology in Transition.* Montreal: Eden Press.

Dutton, D. G. 1987. "Predictors of Recidivism in Convicted Wife Assaulters." Paper presented at the Third National Family Violence Research Conference, Durham, NH.

Fagan, J. 1987. "Cessation of Family Violence: Deterrence and Dissuasion." In L. Ohlin and M. Tonry, eds. *Crime and Justice: An Annual Review of Research.* Chicago: Univ. of Chicago Press.

Gondolf, E. W. Forthcoming. "Changing Men Who Batter: A Developmental Model for Integrated Intervention." *Journal of Family Violence.*

Gondolf, E. W., and J. Hanneken. 1987. "The Gender Warrior: Reformed Batterers on Abuse, Treatment, and Change." *Journal of Family Violence.* 2(2): 177-191.

Hamberger, L. K., and J. E. Hastings. 1986. "Characteristics of Spouse Abusers: Predictors of Treatment Acceptance." *Journal of Interpersonal Violence.* 1(3): 363-373.

Johnston, M. E. 1984. "Correlates of Early Violence Experience Among Men Who Are Abusive Toward Female Mates." Paper presented at the Second National Conference for Family Violence Researchers, Durham, NH.

Ptacek, J. 1984. "Men Who Batter: Recent Research." Paper presented at Second National Conference for Family Violence Researchers, Durham, NH.

Raiha, N. 1982. "Spouse Abuse in the Military Community: Factors Influencing Incidence and Treatment." In M. Roy, ed. *The Abusive Partner.* New York: Van Nostrand Reinhold.

— Sexual Assault —

MARITAL RAPE

Barshis, V. C. 1983. "The Question of Marital Rape." *Women's Studies International Forum.* 6(4): 383-393.

Bidwell, L., and P. White. 1986. "The Family Context of Marital Rape." *Journal of Family Violence.* 1(3): 277-285.

Bowker, L. H. 1983. "Marital Rape: A Distinct Syndrome?" *Social Casework.* 64(6): 34-352.

Drucker, D. 1979. "The Common Law Does Not Support a Marital Rape Exception for Forcible Rape." *Women's Rights Law Review.* 5:181-200.

Finkelhor, D., and K. Yllo. 1980. "Forced Sex in Marriage: A Preliminary Research Report." *Crime and Delinquency.* 28(3): 459-478.

Finkelhor, D., and K. Yllo. 1983. "Rape in Marriage: A Sociological View." In D. Finkelhor et al., eds. *The Dark Side of Families.* Beverly Hills, CA: Sage.

Freeman, M. 1985. "Doing His Best to Sustain the Sanctity of Marriage." In N. Johnson, ed. *Marital Violence.* Boston: Routledge & Kegan Paul.

Frieze, I. H. 1983. "Investigating the Causes and Consequences of Marital Rape." *Signs.* 8:532-553.

Gelles, R. 1977. "Power, Sex, and Violence: The Case of Marital Rape." *Family Coordinator.* 26(4): 339-344.

Groth, A. N., and T. S. Gary. "Marital Rape." *Medical Aspects of Human Sexuality.* 15:122-132.

Hanneke, C. R., N. M. Shields, and G. J. McCall. 1986. "Assessing the Prevalence of Marital Rape." *Journal of Interpersonal Violence.* 1(3): 350-362.

Mettger, Z. 1982. "A Case of Rape: Forced Sex in Marriage." *Response.* 5(2): 1-2, 13-16.

New York University Law Review. 1979. "The Marital Rape Exemption." *New York University Law Review.* 52:306-323.

Russell, D. 1982. *Rape in Marriage.* New York: Macmillan.

Weingcourt, R. 1985. "Wife Rape: Barriers to Identification and Treatment." *American Journal Psychotherapy.* 39(2): 181-192.

Faulk, M. 1977. "Sexual Factors in Marital Violence." *Medical Aspects of Human Sexuality.* October:30-43.

Finkelhor, D., and K. Yllo. 1985. *License to Rape: Sexual Abuse of Wives.* New York: Holt, Rinehart & Winston.

Jeffords, C. R. 1984. "Prosecutorial Discretion in Cases of Marital Rape." *Victimology.* 9(3-4): 85-99.

CHILD SEXUAL ASSAULT

Alter-Reid, K. 1986. "Sexual Abuse of Children: A Review of the Empirical Findings." *Clinical Psychology Review.* 6(4): 249-266.

Araji, S., and D. Finklehor. 1986. "Abusers: A Review of the Research." In D. Finkelhor, ed. *A Sourcebook on Child Sexual Abuse.* Beverly Hills, CA: Sage.

Corwin, D., L. Berliner, G. Goodman, J. Goodwin, and S. White. 1987. "Child Sexual Abuse and Custody Disputes: No Easy Answers." *Journal of Interpersonal Violence.* 2(1): 91-105.

Fein, E., and G. V. Bishop. "Child Sexual Abuse: Treatment for the Offender." *Social Casework.* 68:122-124.

Finkelhor, D. 1984. *Child Sexual Abuse: New Theory and Research.* New York: Free Press.

Janas, C. 1983. "Family Violence and Child Sexual Abuse." *Medical Hypoanalysis.* 4(2): 68-76.

Jones, D., and J. M. McGraw. 1987. "Reliable and Fictitious Accounts of Sexual Abuse to Children." *Journal of Interpersonal Violence.* 2(1): 27-45.

Lystad, M. H. 1982. "Sexual Abuse in the Home: A Review of the Lit-
erature." *International Journal of Family Psychiatry.* 3(1): 3-31.
Sgroi, S. M. 1982. *Handbook of Clinical Intervention in Child Sexual
Abuse.* Lexington, MA: Lexington.
Snowdon, R. 1982. "Working with Incest Offenders: Excuses, Excuses,
Excuses." *Aegis.* 35:56-63.
Steele, B. F. 1978. "The Child Abuser." In I. Kutash, S. Kutash, and L.
Schlesinger, eds. *Violence: Perspectives on Murder and Aggres-
sion.* San Francisco: Jossey-Bass.
Trepper, T. S., and M. J. Barrett, eds. 1986. *Treating Incest: A
Multimodel Systems Perspective.* New York: Haworth Press.
Truesdell, D. L., J. S. McNeil, and J. P. Deschner. 1986. "Incidence of
Wife Abuse in Incestuous Families." *Social Work.* 31:138-140.

RAPE IN GENERAL

Brownmiller, S. 1975. *Against Our Will: Men, Women and Rape.* New
York: Bantam.
Benke, T. 1982. *Men Who Rape: What They Have to Say About Sexual
Violence.* New York: St. Martins.
Burge, S. K. 1983. "Rape: Individual and Family Reactions." In C.
Figley and H. McCubbin, eds. *Stress and the Family: Coping with
Catastrophe.* New York: Brunner/Mazel.
Costin, F., and F. Schwartz. 1987. "Beliefs About Rape and Women's
Roles: A Four-Nation Study." *Journal of Interpersonal Violence.*
2(1): 46-56.
Estrich. S. 1987. *Real Rape.* Cambridge, MA: Harvard University Press.
Greer, G. J., and I. R. Stuart, eds. *The Sexual Aggressor: Current
Perspectives on Treatment.* New York: Van Nostrand Reinhold.
Groth, N. 1979. *Men Who Rape.* New York: Plenum Press.
Murphy, W. D., E. M. Coleman, and M. R. Haynes. 1986. "Factors
Related to Coercive Sexual Behavior in a Nonclinical Sample of
Males." *Violence and Victims.* 1(4): 255-278.
Russell, D. 1984. *Sexual Exploitation: Rape, Child Sexual Abuse, and
Workplace Harassment.* Beverly Hills, CA: Sage.
Scully, D., and J. Marolla. 1984. "Convicted Rapists' Vocabulary of
Motive: Excuses and Justifications." *Social Problems.* 1(5): 531-
544.
Soley, G. 1984. "The Cultural Roots of Sexual Violence." *Sojourners.*
10:1-15.
Tieger, T. 1981. "Self-Rated Likelihood of Raping and the Social Per-
ception of Rape." *Journal of Research in Personality.* 15:147-158.

— Alcohol Abuse —

ALCOHOL AND DOMESTIC VIOLENCE

Bard, M., and J. Zacker. 1974. "Assaultiveness and Alcohol Use in Family Disputes." *Criminology.* 12(3): 281-292.

Bern, E. H. 1985. "Alcohol Use and Spousal Violence: Implications for Social Service Intervention." *Response.* 8:12-14.

Coleman, D., and M. A. Straus. 1983. "Alcohol Abuse and Family Violence." In E. Gottheil et al., eds. *Alcohol, Drug Abuse and Aggression.* Springfield, IL: C. C. Thomas.

Corenblum, B. 1983. "Reaction to Alcohol-Related Marital Violence: Effects of One's Own Abuse Experience and Alcohol Problems in Casual Attributions." *Journal of Studies on Alcohol.* 44(4): 665-674.

Davies, J. L. 1985. "The Role of Alcohol in Family Violence." *Dissertation Abstracts International.* 45(12).

Eberle, P. A. 1982. "Alcohol Abusers and Non-users: A Discriminant Analysis of Differences Between Two Subgroups of Batterers." *Journal of Health and Social Behavior.* 23:260-271.

Famularo, R., K. Stone, and R. Barnum, and R. Wharton. 1986. "Alcoholism and Severe Child Maltreatment." *American Journal of Orthopsychiatry.* 56(3): 481-484.

Flanzer, J. 1982. "Alcohol and Family Violence: Double Trouble." In M. Roy, ed. *The Abusive Partner.* New York: Van Nostrand Reinhold.

Flanzer, J. 1986. "Violence as a Health Problem. The Example of Child Abuse, Family Violence: The Alcohol Connection." Paper presented at Violence in America Conference, Dallas, TX.

Flanzer, J. 1987. "Double Trouble: Alcoholism and Family Violence." In R. J. Ackerman, ed. *Growing in the Shadow: Children of Alcoholics.* Pompano Beach, FL: Health Communications.

Frieze, I. H., and J. Knoble. 1980. "The Effects of Alcohol and Marital Violence." Paper presented at the American Psychological Association, Montreal, Canada.

Hanks, S. E., and C. P. Rosenbaum. 1977. "Battered Women: A Study of Women Who Live With Violent Alcohol-Abusing Men." *American Journal of Orthopsychiatry.* 47:291-306.

Hindman, M. H. 1982. "Family Violence and Alcohol." *The Police Chief.* 49(12): 39-41.

Kantor, G. K., and M. A. Straus. 1986. "The Drunken Bum Theory of Wife Beating." Paper presented at National Alcoholism Forum, San Francisco, CA.

Kantor, G. K., and M. A. Straus. 1986. "Substance Abuse as a Precip-
itant of Family Violence Victimization." Paper presented at the
American Society of Criminology, Atlanta, GA.
Powers, R., and I. Kutash. 1982. "Alcohol, Drugs, and Partner Abuse."
In M. Roy, ed. *The Abusive Partner.* New York: Van Nostrand
Reinhold.
Richardson, D. C., and J. L. Campbell. 1980. "Alcohol and Wife Abuse:
The Effects of Alcohol on Attributions of Blame for Wife
Abuse." *Personality and Social Psychology Bulletin.* 6:51-56.
Van Hasselt, V. B., R. L. Morrison, and A. S. Bellack. 1985. "Alcohol
Abuse in Wife Abusers and Their Spouses." *Addictive Behaviors.*
10:127-135.

EFFECTS OF ALCOHOL ABUSE

Ackerman, R. J. 1987. *Same House, Different Homes: Why Adult Chil-
dren of Alcoholics Are Not All The Same.* Pompano Beach, FL:
Health Communications.
Byles, J. A. 1978. "Violence, Alcohol Problems and Other Problems in
Disintegrating Families." *Journal of Studies on Alcohol.* 39:551-
553.
Coid, J. 1982. "Alcoholism and Violence." *Drug & Alcohol Dependence.*
9(1): 1-13.
Fitzpatrick, J. P. 1974. "Drugs, Alcohol, and Violent Crime." *Addic-
tive Disorders.* 1:353-367.
George, W. H., and G. A. Marlatt. 1986. "The Effects of Alcohol and
Anger on Interest in Violence, Erotica and Deviance." *Journal of
Abnormal Psychology.* 95:150-158.
Gerson, L. W. 1978. "Alcohol-Related Acts of Violence: Who Was
Drinking and Where the Acts Occurred." *Journal of Studies on
Alcohol.* 39:1294-1296.
Hull, J. G., and C. F. Bond. 1986. "Social and Behavioral Consequences
of Alcohol Consumption and Expectancy: A Meta-Analysis." *Psy-
chological Bulletin.* 99:347-360.
Lang, A. R., D. J. Goeckner, V. J. Adesso, and G. A. Marlatt. 1975.
"Effects of Alcohol on Aggression in Male Social Drinkers."
Journal of Abnormal Psychology. 84(5): 508-518.
Leonard, K., E. Bromet, D. Parkison, N. Day, and C. Ryan. 1985.
"Patterns of Alcohol Use and Physically Aggressive Behavior in
Men." *Journal of Studies on Alcohol.* 46:279-282.
Mayfield, D. 1976. "Alcoholism, Alcohol, Intoxication, and Assaultive
Behavior." *Diseases of the Nervous System.* 37:288-291.

Nicol, A. R., J. C. Gunn, J. Gristwood, R. H. Foggit, and J. P. Watson. 1973. "The Relationship of Alcoholism to Violent Behavior Resulting in Long-Term Imprisonment." *British Journal of Psychiatry.* 123:47-51.

Powers, R. J., and I. L. Kutash. 1979 "Substance-Induced Aggression." In I. Kutash et al., eds. *Violence: Perspective on Murder and Aggression.* San Fransico: Jossey-Bass.

Schaef, A. W. 1987. *When Society Becomes an Addict.* New York: Harper & Row.

Sobell, L. C., and M. B. Sobell. 1975. "Drunkness: A 'Special Circumstance' in Crime and Violence, Sometimes." *International Journal of the Addictions.* 10:869-882.

Taylor, S. P., and C. B. Gammon. 1975. "Effects of Type and Dose of Alcohol on Human Physical Aggression." *Journal of Personality and Social Psychology.* 32:169-175.

Vaillant, G. E. 1983. *The Natural History of Alcoholism.* Cambridge, MA: Harvard Univ. Press.

Virkkunen, M. 1974. "Alcohol as a Factor Precipitating Aggression and Conflict Behavior Leading to Homicide." *British Journal of Addictions.* 69:149-154.

Zelchner, A., and R. O. Pihl. 1979. "Effects of Alcohol and Behavior Contingencies on Human Aggression." *Journal of Abnormal Psychology.* 88:153-160.

TREATMENT OF ALCOHOL ABUSE

Bissell, L. 1980. "Diagnosis and Recognition." In S. E. Gitlow, ed. *Alcoholism: A Practical Treatment Guide.* New York: Grune & Stratton.

Blane, H. T. 1977. "Issues in the Evaluation of Alcoholism Treatment." *Professional Psychology.* 8(4): 593-608.

Cavaila, A. A. 1984. "Resistance Issues in the Treatment of DWI Offenders." *Alcoholism Treatment Quarterly.* 1(2): 87-100.

Chernus, L. A. 1985. "Clinical Issues In Alcoholism Treatment." *Social Casework.* 66:67-75.

Christianson, K. E. 1984. "Effects of Cognitive Therapy on Cognitive Expectancy and Alcohol Consumption of Male Problem Drinkers." *Dissertation Abstracts International.* 44(11).

Cox, W. M., ed. 1986. *Treatment and Prevention of Alcohol Problems: A Resource Manual.* Orlando, FL: Academic Press.

Denzin, N. K. 1987. *The Recovering Alcoholic.* Beverly Hills, CA: Sage.

Denzin, N. K. 1987. *Treating Alcoholism.* Beverly Hills, CA: Sage.

Edward, G., J. Orford, S. Egert, S. Guthrie, A. Hawker, C. Hensman, M. Mitcheson, E. Oppenheimer, and C. Taylor. 1977. "Alcoholism: A Controlled Trial of 'Treatment' and 'Advice.'" *Journal of Studies on Alcohol.* 38(5): 1004-1031.

Galanter, M. 1984. "Self-Help Large Group Therapy for Alcoholism: A Controlled Study." *Alcoholism: Clinical and Experimental Research.* 8(1): 16-23.

Icard, L., and D. M. Traunstein. 1987. "Black, Gay, Alcoholic Men: Their Character and Treatment." *Social Casework.* 68:267-272.

Lehman, L., and S. Krupp. 1984. "Alcohol-Related Domestic Violence: Clinical Implications and Intervention Strategies." *Alcoholism Treatment Quarterly.* 1(4): 111-115.

Leikin, C. 1986. "Identifying and Treating the Alcoholic Client." *Social Casework.* 67(2): 67-73.

Marlatt, G. A., and D. M. Donovan. 1982. "Behavioral Psychology Approaches to Alcoholism." In E. M. Pattison and E. Kaufman, eds. *Encyclopedic Handbook of Alcoholism.* New York: Gardner Press.

Marlatt, G. A., and J. Gordon. 1986. *Relapse Prevention.* New York: Guilford.

Potter-Efron, R. T., and P. S. Potter-Efron. 1985. "Family Violence as a Treatment Issue With Chemically Dependent Adolescents." *Alcoholism Treatment Quarterly.* 2(2): 1-15.

Powers, R. J., L. B. Schlesinger, and M. Benson. 1983. "Family Violence: Effects of A Film Program for Alcohol Dependent Persons." *Journal of Drug Education.* 13(2): 153-160.

Stall, R., and P. Biernacki. 1986. "Spontaneous Remissions from the Problematic Use of Substances: An Inductive Model Derived from Comparative Analysis of Alcohol, Opiate, Tobacco, and Food/Obesity Literature. *The International Journal of the Addictions.* 2:1-23.

Winegar, N., T. A. Stephens, and E. D. Varney. 1987. "Alcoholics Anonymous and the Alcoholic Defense Structure." *Social Casework.* 68(4): 223-228.

Intervention with the Batterer

— Treatment Issues —

SAFETY

Gross, D. R., and S. E. Robinson. 1987. "Ethics, Violence, and Counseling: Hear No Evil, See No Evil, and Speak No Evil?" *Journal of Counseling and Development.* 65(7): 340-344.

Hart, B. 1987. *Safety for Women: Monitoring Batterers' Programs.* Harrisburg: Pennsylvania Coalition Against Domestic Violence.

Hart, B. 1987. "Beyond the 'Duty to Warn': A Therapist's 'Duty to Protect' Women and Children." In K. Yllo and M. Bograd, eds. *Feminist Perspectives on Wife Abuse.* Beverly Hills, CA: Sage.

Kaplan, S., and E. Wheeler. 1983. "Survival Skills for Working with Potentially Violent Clients." *Social Casework.* 64(6): 339-346.

Meloy, J. R. 1987. "The Prediction of Violence in Outpatient Psychotherapy." *American Journal of Psychology.* 41(1): 38-45.

Sonkin, D. J. 1986. "Clairvoyance vs. Common Sense: Therapist's Duty to Warn and Protect." *Violence and Victims.* 1(1): 7-20.

Sonkin, D. J., and J. E. Ellison. 1986. "The Therapist's Duty to Protect Victims of Domestic Violence: Where We Have Been and Where We Are Going." *Violence and Victims.* 1(3): 205-213.

Star, B. 1984. "Patient Violence/Therapist Safety." *Social Work.* 29(2): 225-230.

SELF-HELP AND SOCIAL SUPPORT

Balgopal, P. R., P. H. Ephross, T. V. Vassil. 1986. "Self-Help Groups and Professional Helpers." *Small Group Behavior.* 17(2): 123-137.

Bertcher, H. J. 1979. *Group Participation: Techniques for Leaders and Members.* Beverly Hills, CA: Sage

Brownell, A., and S. A. Shumaker. 1984. "Social Support: An Introduction to a Complex Phenomenon." *Journal of Social Issues.* 40(4): 1-9.

Brownell, A., and S. A. Shumaker. 1985. "Where Do We Go From Here? The Policy Implications of Social Support." *Journal of Social Issues.* 41(1): 111-121.

Gottlieb, B. 1981. "Social Networks and Social Support in Community Mental Health." In B. Gottlieb, ed. *Social Networks and Social Support.* Beverly Hills, CA: Sage.

54   Intervention with the Batterer

Heppner, P. 1981. "Counseling Men in Groups." *Personnel and Guidance Journal.* 60(4): 249-252.

Holleb, G., and W. Abrams. 1975. *Alternatives in Community Mental Health: Why Alternative Counseling Centers Started, How They've Fared, Their Future Role.* Boston, MA: Beacon Press.

Kanfer, F. H., and A. P. Goldstein, eds. 1986. *Helping People Change: A Textbook of Methods.* 3d ed. New York: Pergamon.

Madden, D. J. 1986. "Psychotherapeutic Approaches in the Treatment of Violent Persons." In L. Roth, ed. *Clinical Treatment of the Violent Person.* New York: Guilford.

Mallory, L. 1984. *Leading Self-Help Groups: A Guide for Training Facilitators.* New York: Family Service America.

Remine, D., R. M. Rice, and J. Ross. 1980. *Self-Help Groups and Human Service Agencies: How They Work Together.* New York: Family Service America.

Silverman, P. R. 1980. *Mutual Help Groups: Organization and Development.* Beverly Hills, CA: Sage.

Specht, H. "Social Support, Social Networks, Social Exchange, and Social Work Practice." *Social Service Review.* 60:218-240.

Toro, P. A. 1986. "A Comparison of Natural and Professional Help." *American Journal of Community Psychology.* 14:147-159.

Toro, P. A. 1987. "Social Climate Comparison of Mutual Help and Psychotherapy Groups." *Journal of Consulting & Clinical Psychology.* 55(3): 430-431.

Toseland, R. W., and L. Hacker. 1985. "Social Workers' Use of Self-Help Groups as a Resource for Clients." *Social Work.* 30:232-237.

Warren, D. 1981. *Helping Networks: How People Cope With Problems in the Urban Community.* Notre Dame, IN: University of Notre Dame Press.

Whitaker, D. S. 1985. *Using Groups to Help People.* Boston: Routledge & Kegan Paul.

Whittaker, J. K. 1983. "Mutual Helping in Human Service Practice." In J. K. Whittaker and J. Garbarino, eds. *Social Support Networks: Informal Helping in the Human Services.* Hawthorne, NY: Aldine.

TREATMENT AIDS

Anderson, C., and S. Stewart. 1984. *Mastering Resistance: A Practical Guide to Family Therapy.* New York: Guilford.

Anderson, J. 1984. *Counseling Through Group Process.* New York: Springer.

Beck, A. T., A. J. Rush, B. F. Shaw, and G. E. Emery. 1979. *Cognitive Therapy of Depression.* New York: Guilford.

Blasi, A. 1980. "Bridging Moral Cognition and Moral Action: A Critical Review of the Literature." *Psychological Bulletin.* 88:1-45.

Brandell, J. R. 1987. "Focal-Conflict Theory: A Model for Teaching Dynamic Practice." *Social Casework.* 68:299-310.

Fish, R. C., and L. S. Fish. 1986. "Quid Pro Quo Revisted: The Basis of Marital Therapy." *American Journal of Orthopsychiatry.* 56(3): 371-384.

Fredericksen, L. W., and N. Rainwater. 1981. "Explosive Behavior: A Skill Development Treatment Approach." In R. B. Stuart, ed. *Violent Behavior: Social Learning Approaches to Prediction, Management and Treatment.* New York: Brunner/Mazel.

Gelles, R. 1982. "Applying Research on Family Violence to Clinical Practice." *Journal of Marriage and the Family.* 44(1): 9-19.

Hartman, C., and D. Reynolds. 1987. "Resistant Clients: Confrontation, Interpretation, and Alliance." *Social Casework.* 68(4): 205-213.

Hewstone, M. 1971. *The Transparent Self.* Revised ed. New York: Van Nostrand Reinhold.

Hocker, J., and W. Wilmot. 1985. *Interpersonal Conflict.* 2d ed. Dubuque, IA: William C. Brown.

Kanfer, F. H., and A. P. Goldstein, eds. 1986. *Helping People Change: A Textbook of Methods.* 3d ed. New York: Pergamon.

Novaco, R. W. 1975. *Anger Control: The Development and Evaluation of an Experimental Treatment (Anger Scale).* Lexington, MA: Lexington.

Pinderhughes, E. B. 1983. "Empowerment for Our Clients and for Ourselves." *Social Casework.* 64:331-338.

Scher, M., M. Stevens, G. Eichenfeld, and G. Good. 1987. *Handbook for Counseling Men.* Beverly Hills, CA: Sage.

Sigel, I. E., and L. M. Laosa. 1983. *Changing Families.* New York: Plenum Press.

Thackrey, M. 1986. *Therapeutics for Aggression: Pyschological/ Physical Crisis Intervention.* New York: Human Sciences Press.

Thorman, G. 1982. *Helping Troubled Families: A Social Work Perspective.* Hawthorne, NY: Aldine.

Toseland, R. W. 1987. "Treatment Discontinuance: Grounds for Optimism." *Social Casework.* 68:195-205.

Van Hasselt, V. B., A. S. Bellack, R. O. Morrison, and M. Hersen, eds. 1986. *Handbook of Family Violence.* New York: Plenum Press.

Walsh, J. A. 1987. "Burnout and Values in the Social Service Profession." *Social Casework.* 68:279-286.

Zuk, G. H. 1986. *Process and Practice in Family Therapy.* 2d ed. New York: Human Sciences Press.

RACE AND OTHER ISSUES

Bowen, N. H. 1987. "Pornography: Research Review and Implications for Counseling." *Journal of Counseling and Development.* 65(7): 345-350.

Delgado, M. 1983. "Hispanics and Psychotherapeutic Groups." *International Journal of Group Psychotherapy.* 33:507-520.

Delgado, M., and D. Humm-Delgado. 1982. "Natural Support Systems: A Source of Strengths in Hispanic Communities." *Social Work.* 27:83-89.

Figley, C. R., ed. 1985. *Trauma and Its Wake: The Study of Treatment of Post-Traumatic Stress Disorder.* New York: Brunner/Mazel.

Gwartney-Gibbs, P. A., J. Stockard, and S. Bohmer. 1987. "Learning Courtship Aggression: The Influence of Parents, Peers, and Personal Experiences." *Family Relations.* 36:276-282.

Greer, J., and I. Stuart, eds. 1983. *The Sexual Aggressor: Current Perspectives on Treatment.* New York: Van Nostrand Reinhold.

Hampton, R., ed. Forthcoming. *Domestic Violence and the Black Family.* Lexington, MA: Lexinton.

Hardy-Fanta, C. 1986. "Social Action in Hispanic Groups." *Social Work.* 31:119-123.

Ho, M. K. 1987. *Family Therapy with Ethnic Minorities.* Beverly Hills, CA: Sage.

Humm-Delgado, D., and M. Delgado. 1986. "Gaining Community Entree to Assess Service Needs of Hispanics." *Social Casework.* 67:80-87.

Jones, R. 1983. "Increasing Staff Sensitivity to the Black Client." *Social Casework.* 63:418-426.

Koch, A., and T. Ingram. 1985. "The Treatment of Borderline Personality Disorder within a Distressed Relationship." *Journal of Marital and Family Therapy.* 11(4): 373-380.

Leashore, B. 1981. "Social Services and Black Men." In L. Gary, ed. *Black Men.* Beverly Hills, CA: Sage.

Long, K. A. "Cultural Considerations in the Assessment and Treatment of Intrafamilial Abuse." *American Journal of Orthopsychiatry.* 56(1): 131-136.

Martin, J. M., and E. P. Martin. 1985. *The Helping Tradition in the Black Family and Community.* Silver Springs, MD: National Association of Social Workers.

Martinez, C. 1977. "Group Process and the Chicano: Clinical Issues." *International Journal of Group Psychotherapy.* 27:225-231.

Penk, W., and R. Robinowitz. 1987. "Post-Traumatic Stress Disorders (PTSD) Among Vietnam Veterans." *Journal of Clinical Psychology.* 43(1): 3-5.

Saltzman, A. "Reporting Child Abusers and Protecting Substance Abusers." *Social Work.* 31:474-475.

Scher, M. 1981. "Men Hiding: A Challenge for the Counselor." *Personnel and Guidance Journal.* 60(4): 199-203.

Solkoff, N., P. Gray, and S. Keill. 1986. "Which Vietnam Veterans Develop Posttraumatic Stress Disorder?" *Journal of Clinical Psychology.* 42(5): 607-698.

Stanback, H. 1981. "A Black Historical Perspective." In E. Mizio and A. J. Delaney, eds. *Training for Service Delivery to Minority Clients.* New York: Family Services of America.

Yoken, C., and J. S. Berman. 1984. "Does Paying for Psychotherapy Alter the Effectiveness of Treatment?" *Journal of Consulting & Clinical Psychology.* 52(2): 254-260.

PRIORITIES

Adams, D. 1987. "A Profeminist Analysis of Treatment Models of Men Who Batter." In K. Yllo and M. Bograd, eds. *Feminist Perspectives on Wife Abuse.* Beverly Hills, CA: Sage.

Brennan, A. F. 1983. "Political and Psychosocial Issues in Psychotherapy for Spouse Abusers: Implications for Treatment." Paper presented at the American Psychological Association, Anaheim.

Busch, K. 1982. "New Roles for Men and Their Groups in the Battered Women's Movement." Paper presented at The Visions Forum of the Pennsylvania Coalition Against Domestic Violence, Pottstown, PA.

Edleson, J. 1984. "Violence is the Issue: A Critique of Neidig's Assumptions." *Victimology.* 9(3-4): 483-489.

Gondolf, E. W. Under review. "Batterer Counseling and Shelter Outcome: An Empirical Study of Planned Living Arrangements." *Journal of Interpersonal Violence.*

Gondolf, E. W., and D. Russell. 1986. "The Case Against Anger Control Treatment Programs for Batterers." *Response.* 9(3): 2-5.

McLaughlin, L. 1982. "Children and Women First." Paper presented at the Visions Forum of Pennsylvania Coalition Against Domestic Violence, Pottstown, PA.

Morrison, M. 1982. "Seem Angry? I am Angry!" *Aegis.* 36:17-25.

Neidig, P. H. 1984. "Women's Shelters, Men's Collectives, and Other Factors in the Treatment of Spouse Abuse." *Victimology.* 9(3-4): 464-476.

Pence, E. 1987. "Making Social Change: The Dynamics of Education, Action and Reflection." *Aegis.* 42:5-8.

Summers, G., and N. S. Feldman. 1984. "Blaming the Victim versus Blaming the Perpetrator: An Attributional Analysis of Spouse Abuse." *Journal of Social Clinical Psychology.* 2(4): 339-347.

— Men's Programs —

SUPERVISED GROUPS

Bern, Elliot H. and Linda L. Bern. 1984. "A Group Program for Men Who Commit Violence Towards Their Wives." *Social Work with Groups.* 7(1): 63-76.

Boyd, V. 1978. "Domestic Violence: Treatment Alternatives for the Male Batterer." Paper presented at the American Psychological Association, Toronto, Canada.

Brygger, M. P., and J. L. Edleson. In press. "The Domestic Abuse Project: A Multi-Systems Intervention in Woman Battering." *Journal of Interpersonal Violence.*

Currie, D. W. 1983. "Treatment Groups for Violent Men: A Toronto Model." *Social Work with Groups.* 6(4): 179-188.

Deschner, J. P., J. S. McNeil, and M. G. Moore, 1986. "A Treatment Model for Batterers." *Social Casework.* 67(1): 55-60.

Edleson, J. 1984. "Working with Men Who Batter." *Social Work.* 29:237-242.

Garent, S., and D. Moss. 1982. "How to Set Up a Counseling Program for Self-Referred Batterers: The AWAIC Model." In M. Roy, ed. *The Abusive Partner: An Analysis of Domestic Battering.* New York: Van Nostrand Reinhold.

Hall, R., and L. Ryan. 1984. "Therapy with Men Who Are Violent with Their Spouses." *Australian Journal of Family Therapy.* 5(4): 281-282.

Halpern, M. 1983. "Treatment of the Male Batterer: The BWA Program." Paper presented at the 91st Annual Convention of the American Psychological Association, Anaheim, CA.

Hamberger, L. K. 1984. "Helping Men Who Batter: A Two Stage Community Intervention Program." Paper presented at the American Psychological Association, Toronto, Canada.

Koval, J. E., J. J. Ponzetti, and R. M. Cane. 1983. "Programmatic Intervention for Men Involved in Congual Violence." *Family Therapy.* 9(2): 147-154.

Long, D. 1987. "Working With Men Who Batter." In M. Scher et al. *Handbook for Counseling and Psychotherapy with Men.* Beverly Hills, CA: Sage.

Mott-McDonald Associates. 1981. *The Report from the Conference on Prevention Programs for Men Who Batter.* Washington, DC: GPO.

Murphy, W. A. 1984. " A Military Anger Management Program for Men Who Batter." Paper presented at the American Psychological Association, Toronto, Canada.

Myers, T., and S. Gilbert. 1983. "Wifebeater's Group Through a Women's Center: Why and How." *Victimology.* 8(1-2): 238-248.

Nikstaitis, G. 1985. "Therapy for Men Who Batter: An Interview." *Journal of Psychosocial Nursing.* 23:33-36.

Pence, E. 1983. "The Duluth Domestic Abuse Intervention Project." *Hamiline Law Review.* 6:247-275.

Russell, D. 1985. "Facing Up to Spouse Abuse: A Theme-Centered Program for Batterers." Unpublished paper. Pittsburgh, PA: Second Step Program.

Saunders, D. 1982. "Counseling the Violent Husband." In P.A. Keller and L. G. Ritt, eds. *Innovations in Clinical Practice: A Source Book,* Volume 1. Sarasota, FL: Professional Resource Exchange.

Saunders, D. 1984. "Helping Husbands Who Batter." *Social Casework.* 64:347-353.

Scher, M., and M. Stevens. 1987. "Men and Violence." *Journal of Counseling and Development.* 65(7): 351-356.

Sonkin, D. J., D. Martin, and L. Walker. 1985. *The Male Batterer: A Treatment Approach.* New York: Springer.

Steinfeld, G. J. 1986. "Spouse Abuse: Clinical Implications of Research on the Control Aggression." *Journal of Family Violence.* 1(2): 197-208.

Waldo, M. 1986. "Group Counseling for Military Personnel Who Batter Their Wives." *Journal for Specialists in Group Work.* 11:132-138.

Waldo., M. 1985. "Curative Factor Framework for Conceptualizing Group Counseling." *Journal of Counseling and Development.* 64:132-138.

NOTE: Also see section entitled *Program Manuals* for books and monographs on men's programs.

MANDATED COUNSELING

Dreas, G., D. Ignatov, and T. Brennan, 1982. "The Male Batterer: A Model Treatment Program for the Courts." *Federal Probation.* 46(4): 50-55.

Finn, J. Forthcoming. "Men's Domestic Violence Treatment: The Court Referral Component." *Journal of Interpersonal Violence.*

Ganley, A. L. 1987. "Perpetrators of Domestic Violence: Counseling the Court Mandated Client." In D. J. Sonkin, ed. *Domestic Violence on Trial: Psychological and Legal Dimensions of Family Violence.* New York: Springer.

Reilly, P., and R. J. Grusznski. 1984. "A Structured Didactic Model for Men Controlling Family Violence." *International Journal of Offender Therapy and Comparative Criminology.* 28:223-235.

Sonkin, D. J. 1987. "Assessment of Court Mandated Male Batterers." In D. J. Sonkin, ed. *Domestic Violence on Trial: Psychological and Legal Dimensions of Family Violence.* New York: Springer.

Waldo, M. 1987. "Also Victims: Understanding and Treating Men Arrested for Spouse Abuse." *Journal of Counseling and Development.* 65(7): 385-390.

— Couples Counseling —

FAMILY THERAPY

Ball, M. 1977. "Issues of Violence in Family Casework." *Social Casework.* 58:3-12.

Baucom, D. H., and P. A. Aiken. 1984. "Sex Role Identity, Marital Satisfaction and Response to Behavioral Marital Therapy." *Journal of Consulting & Clinical Psychology.* 52:438-444.

Blackie, S., and D. Clark. 1987. "Men in Marriage Counselling." In C. Lewis and M. O'Brien, eds. *Reassessing Fatherhood.* Beverly Hills, CA: Sage.

Bograd, M. 1984. "Family Systems Approaches to Wife Battering: A Feminist Critique." *American Journal of Orthopsychiatry*. 54(4): 558-568.

Bolton, F. G., and S. R. Bolton. 1986. *Working with the Violent Family*. Beverly Hills, CA: Sage.

Buckley, L. B., D. Miller, and T. A. Rolfe. 1983. "Treatment Groups for Violent Men: A Windsor Model." *Social Work with Groups*. 6(4): 189-195.

Cantoni, L. 1981. "Clinical Issues in Domestic Violence." *Social Casework*. 62(1): 3-12.

Feldman, L. B. 1982. "Dysfunctional Marital Conflict: An Integrative Interpersonal-Intrapersonal Model." *Journal of Marital and Family Therapy*. 8:417-428.

Gelles, R. J., and P. E. Maynard. 1987. "A Structural Family Systems Approach to Intervention in Cases of Family Violence." *Family Relations*. 36:270-275.

Guillebeaux, F., C. L. Storm, and A. Semaris. 1986. "Luring the Reluctant Male: A Study of Male Participation in Marriage and Family Therapy." *Family Therapy*. 8(2): 215-225.

Margolin, G. 1979 "Conjoint Marital Therapy to Enhance Anger Management and Reduce Spouse Abuse." *American Journal of Family Therapy*. 7(2) :13-23.

Rice, D. G. 1978. "The Male Spouse in Marital and Family Therapy." *Counseling Psychologist*. 7:64-66.

Taylor, J. W. 1984. "Structured Conjoint Therapy for Spouse Abuse Cases." *Social Casework*. 63:11-18.

Weidman, A. 1986. "Family Therapy With Violent Couples." *Social Casework*. 66:212-218.

Weitzman, J., and K. Dreen. 1982. "Wife Beating: A View of the Marital Dyad." *Social Casework*. 63:259-265.

SPECIALIZED TREATMENT

Bedrosian, R. C. 1982. "Using Cognitive and Systems Intervention in the Treatment of Marital Violence." *Family Therapy Collections*. 3:35-39.

Berghorn, G., and A. Siracusa. 1982. "Beyond Isolated Treatment: A Case for Community Involvement in Family Violence Interventions." *Family Therapy Collections*. 3:139-157.

Bograd, M. 1986. "Holding the Line: Confronting the Abusive Partner." *Family Therapy Networker*. 10(4): 44-47.

Cook, D., and A. Frantz-Cook. 1984. "A Systematic Treatment Approach to Wife Battering." *Journal of Marriage and Family Therapy.* 10:83-93.

Geller, J. 1978. "Reaching the Battering Husband." *Social Work with Groups.* 1(1): 27-37.

Geller, J. 1982. "Conjoint Therapy: Staff Training and Treatment of the Abuser and the Abused." In M. Roy, ed. The Abusive Partner. New York: Van Nostrand Reinhold.

Holmes, S. A. 1981. "A Holistic Approach to the Treatment of Violent Families." *Social Casework.* 62(10): 594-600.

Neidig, P., D. Friedman, and B. Collins. 1985. "Domestic Conflict Containment: A Spouse Abuse Treatment Program." *Social Case work.* 66:195-204.

Reid, J. B., P. S. Taplin, and R. Lorber. 1981. "A Social-Actional Approach to Treatment of Abusive Families." In R. B. Stuart, ed. *Violent Behavior: Social Learning Approaches to Prediction, Management and Treatment.* New York: Brunner/Mazel.

Taylor, J. 1984. "Structured Conjoint Therapy for Spouse Abuse Cases." *Social Casework.* 64:11-18.

Wodarski. J. S. 1981. "Treatment of Parents Who Abuse Their Children: A Literature Review and Implications for Professionals." *Child Abuse and Neglect.* 5:351-360.

— Surveys, Evaluations and Assessments —

PROGRAM SURVEYS

Browning, J. J. 1983. *Stopping the Violence: Canadian Programmes for Assaultive Men.* Ottawa, Canada: Clearinghouse on Family Violence, Health, and Welfare.

Eddy, M., and T. Myers. 1984. "Helping Men Who Batter: Profile of Programs in the United States." Paper presented at the Second National Conference for Family Violence Researchers, Durham, NH.

Feazell, C. S., R. Mayers, and J. Deschner. 1984. "Services for Men Who Batter: Implications for Programs and Policies." *Family Relations.* 33:217-223.

Finn, J. 1985. "Men's Domestic Violence Treatment Groups: A State-wide Survey." *Social Work with Groups.* 8(3): 81-95.

Matsakis-Scarato, A. 1980. "Spouse Abuse Treatment: An Overview." *Aegis.* Winter/Spring:39-48.

Mettger, Z. 1982. "Help for Men Who Batter: An Overview of Issues and Programs." *Response.* 5(6): 1,2,7,8,23.

Pfouts, J. H. 1981. "The Future of Wife Abuser Programs." *Social Work.* 25(6): 451-460.

Pirog-Good, M. A., and J. Stets-Kealey. 1985. "Male Batterers and Battering Prevention Programs: A National Survey." *Response.* 8(3): 8-12.

Pirog-Good, M. A., and J. Stets-Kealey. 1986. "Programs For Abusers: Who Drops Out and What Can Be Done." *Response.* 9(2): 17-19.

Pirog-Good, M. A., and J. Stets-Kealey. In press. "Recidivism in Programs for Abusers." *Victimology.* 11(2).

Roberts, A. 1982. "A National Survey of Services for Batterers." In M. Roy, ed. *The Abusive Partner.* New York: Van Nostrand Reinhold.

Roberts, A. 1984. "Intervention with the Abusive Partner." In A. Roberts, ed. *Battered Women and Their Families.* New York: Springer.

Watts, D., and C. Courtois. 1981. "Trends in the Treatment of Men Who Commit Violence Against Women." *Personnel and Guidance Journal.* 60(4): 244-249.

PROGRAM EVALUATIONS

Deschner, J. P., and J. S. McNeil. 1986. "Results of Anger Control Training for Battering Couples." *Journal of Family Violence.* 1(2): 111-120.

Douglas, M. A., and S. Perrin. 1987. "Follow-up Evaluation for Treatment of Court-Ordered Male Batterers." Paper presented at the Third National Family Violence Research Conference, Durham, NH.

Dutton, D. G. 1986. "The Outcome of Court-Mandated Treatment for Wife Assault: A Quasi-Experimental Evaluation." *Victims and Violence.* 1(3): 163-175.

Edleson, J., and R. Grusznski. In press. "Treating Men Who Batter: Four Years of Outcome Data From the Domestic Abuse Project." *Journal of Social Science Research.*

Edleson, J. L., M. P. Brygger, and M. Syers. 1987. "Comparative Effectiveness of Group Treatment for Men Who Batter: A Midpoint Progress Report." Paper presented at the Third National Family Violence Research Conference, Durham, NH.

Gondolf, E. W. 1987. "Evaluating Programs for Men Who Batter: Problems and Prospects." *Journal of Family Violence.* 2(1): 95-108.

Gondolf, E. W. Forthcoming. "How Some Men Stop Their Abuse: A Preliminary Program Evaluation." In G. Hotaling et al., eds. *New Directions in Family Violence Research.* Beverly Hills, CA: Sage.

Gordon, S., and M. Waldo. 1984. "The Effects of Assertiveness Training on Couples' Relationships." *American Journal of Family Therapy.* 12(1): 73-77.

Hawkins, R. C. and C. Beauvis. 1985. "Evaluation of Group Therapy with Abusive Men: Police Records." Paper presented at the American Psychological Association, Los Angeles, CA.

Hazaleus, S. L., and J. L. Deffenbacker. 1986. "Relaxation and Cognitive Treatments of Anger." *Journal of Consulting & Clinical Psychology.* 54(2): 212-226.

Lindquist, C. U., and C. F. Telch. 1983. "Evaluation of a Conjugal Violence Treatment Programs: A Pilot Study." *Behavioral Counseling/Community Intervention.* 3(1): 76-90.

Lund, S. H., N. E. Larsen, and S. K. Schultz. 1982. "Exploratory Evaluation of the Domestic Abuse Project." Unpublished. Domestic Abuse Project, Minneapolis, MN.

Neidig, P. 1986. "The Development and Evaluation of a Spouse Abuse Treatment Program in a Military Setting." *Evaluation and Program Planning.* 9(3): 275-280.

Rosenbaum, A. 1986. "Group Treatment of Wife Abusers: Process and Outcome." Paper presented at the American Psychological Association, Washington, DC.

Saunders, D. G., and D. Hanusa. 1986. "Cognitive-Behavioral Treatment of Men Who Batter: The Short-Term Effects of Group Therapy." *Journal of Family Violence.* 1(4): 357-369.

Shupe, A., W. Stacey, and L. Hazelwood. 1987. *Violent Men, Violent Couples: The Dynamics of Domestic Violence.* Lexington, MA: Lexington.

Stermac, L. E. 1986. "Anger Control Treatment for Forensic Patients." *Journal of Interpersonal Violence.* 1(4): 446-457.

Tolman, R., M. S. Beeman, and C. Mendoza. 1987. "The Effectiveness of Shelter-Based Structured Group Intervention for Men Who Batter." Paper presented at the Third National Family Violence Research Conference, Durham, NH.

ASSESSMENT INSTRUMENTS

Arias, I., and S. R. Beach. 1987. "Validity of Self-Reports of Marital Violence." *Journal of Family Violence.* 2(2): 139-150.

Barling, J., K. D. O'Leary, E. Jouriles, D. Vivan, and K. E. MacEwen. 1987. "Factor Similarity of the Conflict Tactics Scales Across Samples, Spouses, and Sites: Issues and Implications." *Journal of Family Violence.* 2(1): 37-54.

Baucom, D. H. 1976. "Independent Masculinity and Femininity Scale on the California Psychological Inventory." *Journal of Consulting & Clinical Psychology.* 45:145-155.

Beck, A. T. 1978. *Depression Inventory.* Philadelphia: Center for Cognitive Behavior.

Beck, A. T., M. Kovacs, and A. Wissman. 1979. "Assessment of Suicidal Intention: The Scale for Suicidal Ideation." *Journal of Consulting & Clinical Psychology.* 47(2): 343-352.

Beck, A.T., et al. 1961. "An Inventory for Measuring Depression." *Archives of General Psychiatry.* 4:54-63.

Biderman, A. D. 1981. "Sources of Data for Victimology." *Journal of Criminal Law and Criminology.* 72(2): 789-817.

Bem, S. L. 1974. "The Measurement of Psychological Androgyny (BEM Sex-Roles Test)." *Journal of Consulting & Clinical Psychology.* 42:155-162.

Bower, A. M. 1986. "Behavior Changes in Psychotherapy Groups: A Study Using an Empirically Based Statistical Method." *Small Group Behavior.* 17(2): 164-185.

Brekke, J. S. 1987. "Detecting Wife and Child Abuse in Clinical Settings." *Social Casework.* 68:332-338.

Browning, J. J., and D. Dutton. 1986. "Assessment of Wife Assault with the Conflict Tactics Scale: Using Couple Data to Quantify the Differential Reporting Effect." *Journal of Marriage and the Family.* 48(2): 375-379.

Deschner, J. P., and L. Isbister. In press. "Measuring Family Violence with the Fighting Methods Inventory." *Victimology.* 12(1).

Filsinger, E. E. 1983. *Marriage and Family Assessment: A Sourcebook for Family Therapy.* Beverly Hills, CA: Sage.

Forman, B. D. 1982. "A Substance Abuse Screening Check List." In P. A. Keller and L. G. Ritt, eds. *Innovations in Clinical Practice: A Source Book,* Volume 1. Sarasota, FL: Professional Resource Exchange.

Greenwald, H. J., and Y. Satow. 1970. "A Short Social Desirability Scale." *Psychological Reports.* 27:131-135.

Groves, R. M., and R. L. Kahn. 1979. *Surveys by Telephone: A National Comparison with Personal Interviews.* New York: Academic Press.

Hathaway, S. R., and J. C. McKinley. 1976. *The Minnesota Multiphasic Personal Inventory Manual (MMPI).* New York: Psychological Corporation.

Hedlund, B. L., and C. U. Lindquist. 1984. "The Development of an Inventory for Distinguishing among Passive, Aggressive, and Assertive Behavior." *Behavioral Assessment.* 6:379-390.

Hudson, W. W., and S. R. McIntosh. 1981. "The Assessment of Spouse Abuse: Two Quantifiable Dimensions (SAI)." *Journal of Marriage and the Family.* 43(4): 873-885.

Lachar, D. 1978. *The MMPI: Clinical Assessment and Automated Interpretation.* Los Angles: Western Psychological Services.

Lewis, B. 1985. "The Wife Abuse Inventory: A Screening Device for the Identification of Abused Women." *Social Work.* 30(1): 32-35.

Maiuro, R., P. Vitaliano, and T. Cahn. Forthcoming. "A Brief Measure for the Assessment of Anger and Aggression." *Journal of Interpersonal Violence.*

Marcus, A. C., and L. A. Crane. 1986. "Telephone Surveys in Public Health Research." *Medical Care.* 24:97-112.

Mehrabian, A., and N. Epstein. 1972. "A Measure of Emotional Empathy." *Journal of Personality.* 40:525-543.

Milner, J., and R. Gold. 1986. "Screening Spouse Abusers for Child Abuse Potential." *Journal of Clinical Psychology.* 42(1): 169-172.

Nowicki, S., and M. Duke. 1974. "A Locus of Control Scale for College As Well As Non-College Adults." *Journal of Personality Assessment.* 38:136-137.

O'Leary, K. D., ed. 1978. *Assessment of Marital Discord: An Integration for Research and Clinical Practice.* Hillsdale, NJ: Laurence Erlbaum.

Saunders, D. G., A. B. Lynch, and M. Grayson. 1987. "The Inventory of Beliefs About Wife-Beating: The Construction and Initial Validation of a Measure of Beliefs and Attitudes." *Violence and Victims.* 2(1): 39-58.

Selzer, M. , A. Vinokur, and L. VanRooijen. 1975. " A Self-Administered Short Michigan Alcoholism Screening Test (SMAST)." *Journal of Studies in Alcohol.* 36:117-126.

Selzer, M. 1971. "The Michigan Alcoholism Screening Test: The Quest for a New Diagnostic Instrument (MAST)." *American Journal of Psychiatry.* 127:1653-1658.

Shelton, J., J. Hollister, and E. Gocka. 1969. "Quantifying Alcoholic Impairment (Impairment Index)." *Modern Medicine.* 37:188-189.

Spanier, G. B. 1976. "Measuring Dyadic Adjustment: New Scales for Assessing the Quality of Marriage and Similar Dyads." *Journal of Marriage and the Family.* 38:15-28.

Spence, J. T., and R. L. Helmreich. 1978. *Masculinity and Femininity: Their Psychological Dimensions, Correlates and Antecedents.* Austin: University of Texas.

Spence, J. T., R. L. Helmreich, and J. Stapp. 1974. *The Personal Attributes Questionnaire: A Measure of Sex-Role Stereotypes and Masculinity-Femininity. Journal Supplement Abstract Service, Catalog Documents Psychology.* 4 (Ms. No. 127).

Spence, J., and W. Helmreich. 1972. "The Attitudes Toward Women's Scale: An Objective Instrument to Measure Attitudes Toward the Rights and Roles of Women in Contemporary Society." *Journal Supplement Abstract Service,* Catalog of Selected Documents in Psychology. 2 (Ms. No. 153).

Straus, M. A. 1979. "Measuring Intrafamily Conflict and Violence: The Conflict Tactics (CT) Scales." *Journal of Marriage and the Family.* 41:75-88.

Tolman, R. M. 1987. "The Development and Validation of a Scale of Non-Physical Abuse." Paper presented at the Third National Family Violence Research Conference, Durham, NH.

EVALUATION AND ASSESSMENT ISSUES

Brown, J. 1987. "A Review of Meta-Analysis Conducted on Psychotherapy Outcome Research." *Clinical Psychology Review.* 7(1): 1-23.

Bordin, E. S. 1986. "The Effectiveness of Psyhotherapy: An Introduction." *American Journal of Orthopsychiatry.* 56(4): 500-512.

DeMaris, A., and J. Jackson. 1986. "Nonrespondent Characteristics and Bias in a Study of Batterers." *Social Service Review.* 60:461-474.

Edleson, J. L., and M. P. Brygger. 1986. "Gender Differences in Reporting Battering Incidences." *Family Relations.* 35:377-382.

Gelles, R. J. 1978. "Methods for Studying Sensitive Family Topics." *American Journal of Orthopsychiatry.* 48(3): 408-424.

Gondolf, E. W. 1987. "Evaluating Programs for Men Who Batter: Problems and Prospects." *Journal of Family Violence.* 2(1): 95-108.

Gondolf, E. W. Forthcoming. "Seeing Through Smoke and Mirrors: A Guide to Batterer Program Evaluations." *Response.*

Greenberg, L. S. 1986. "Change Process Research." *Journal of Consulting & Clinical Psychology.* 54(1): 4-9.

Hanneke, C. R., and N. M. Shields. 1981. "Patterns of Family and Non-Family Violence: An Approach to the Study of Violent Husbands." Paper presented at the National Conference for Family Violence Researchers, Durham, NH.

Ivanoff, A., B. J. Blythe, and S. Briar. 1987. "The Empirical Clinical Practice Debate." *Social Casework.* 68:290-298.

Jouriles, E. N., and K. D. O'Leary. 1985. "Interpersonal Reliability of Reports of Marital Violence." *Journal of Consulting & Clinical Psychology.* 53(3): 419-421.

Lockhart, L. L. 1985. "Methodological Issues in Comparative Racial Analysis: The Case of Wife Abuse." *Social Work Research and Abstracts.* 21(2): 35-41.

Olin, R. J. 1986. "Program Evaluation in a Family Service Agency." *Social Casework.* 67:108-114.

Porter, S. J. 1986. "Assessment: A Vital Process in the Treatment of Family Violence." *Family Therapy.* 13(1): 105-112.

Saunders, D. G. 1984. "Issues in Conducting Treatment Research with Men Who Batter." Paper presented at the Second National Conference for Family Violence Researchers, Durham, NH.

Sherman, L. 1984. "Randomized Field Experiments in Domestic Violence Research." Paper presented at the Second National Conference for Family Violence Researchers, Durham, NH.

Straus, M. A., 1981. "Protecting Human Subjects: The Case of Family Violence." In E. E. Filsinger and R. A. Lewis, eds. *Assessing Marriage: New Behavioral Approaches.* Beverly Hills: Sage.

Szinovacz, M. 1983. "Using Couple Data as a Methodological Tool: The Case of Marital Violence." *Journal of Marriage and the Family.* 45(3): 633-643.

Van Hasselt, V. B., J. Milliones, and M. Hersen. 1981. "Behavioral Assessment of Drug Addiction: Strategies and Issues in Research and Treatment." *International Journal of the Addictions.* 16:43-68.

Weis, J. G. 1987. Issues in Family Violence Research Methodology and Design. In L. Ohlin and M. Tonry, eds. *Crime and Justice: An Annual Review of Research.* Chicago: Univ. of Chicago Press.

Yllo, K. 1983. "Using a Feminist Approach in Quantitative Research." In D. Finkelhor et al., eds. *The Dark Side of Families.* Beverly Hills, CA: Sage.

— Police and Community Intervention —

POLICE ACTION

Bell, D. J. 1985. "A Multiyear Study of Ohio Urban and Rural Police Disposition of Domestic Disputes." *Victimology*. 10(1-4): 300-310.

Berk, R. A., and P. J. Newton. 1985. "Does Arrest Really Deter Wife Battery? An Effort to Replicate the Findings of the Minneapolis Spouse Abuse Experiment." *American Sociological Review*. 50:253-262.

Berk, R. A., D. R. Loseke, S. F. Berk, and D. Rauma. 1980. "Bringing the Cops Back In: A Study of Efforts to Make the Criminal Justice System More Responsive to Incidents of Family Violence." *Social Science Research*. 9:193-215.

Berk, S., and D. Loseke. 1981. Handling Family Violence: Situational Determinants of Police Arrest in Domestic Disturbances." *Law and Society Review*. 15(2): 317-344.

Bowker, L. H. 1984. "Battered Wives and the Police: A National Study of Usage and Effectiveness." *Police Studies*. 7:84-93.

Carr, J. 1982. "Treating Family Abuse Using a Police Crisis Team Approach." In M. Roy, ed. *The Abusive Partner*. New York: Van Nostrand Reinhold.

Davis, P. W. 1983. "Restoring the Semblance of Order: Police Strategies in the Domestic Disturbance." *Symbolic Interaction*. 6(2): 216-274.

Dolon, R., J. Hendricks, and M. S. Meagher. 1986. "Police Practices and Attitudes Toward Domestic Violence." *Journal of Police Science and Administration*. 14(3): 187-192.

Dutton, D. G. Forthcoming. *The Domestic Assault of Women: Psychological and Criminal Justice Perspectives*. Newton, MA: Allyn & Bacon.

Erez, E. 1986. "Intimacy, Violence, and the Police." *Human Relations*. 39(3): 265-281.

Ferraro, K. J. 1985. "Protecting Women: Police and Battering." Paper presented at the American Sociological Association, Washington, DC.

Gondolf, E. W. Under review. "Handling Anti-Social Men: The Police Action in Wife Abuse Cases. *Criminal Justice and Behavior*.

Hanewicz, W., C. Cassidy-Rislee, L. Fransway, and M. O'Neill. 1982. "Improving the Linkages Between Domestic Violence Referral Agencies and the Police: A Research Note." *Journal of Criminal Justice*. 10:493-503.

Homant, R. J., and D. B. Kennedy. 1985. "Police Perceptions of Spouse Abuse: A Comparison of Male and Female Officers." *Journal of Criminal Justice.* 13(1): 29-47.

Humphreys, J. C., and W. O. Humphreys. 1985. "Mandatory Arrest: A Means of Primary and Secondary Prevention of Abuse of Female Partners." *Victimology.* 10(1-4): 267-280.

Jaffe, P., D. A. Wolfe, A. Telford, and G. Austin. 1986. "The Impact of Police Charges in Incidents of Wife Abuse." *Journal of Family Violence.* 1(1): 37-49.

Pearce, J. B., and J. R. Snortum. 1983. "Police Effectiveness in Handling Disturbance Calls." *Criminal Justice and Behavior.* 10(1): 71-92.

Police Foundation. 1976. *Domestic Violence and the Police: Studies in Detroit and Kansas City.* Washington, DC: Police Foundation.

Radford, J. 1987. "Policing Male Violence -- Policing Women." In J. Hanmer and M. Maynard, eds. *Women, Violence, and Social Control.* London: Macmillan.

Saunders, D. G. and P. B. Size. 1986. "Attitudes About Woman Abuse Among Police Officers, Victims, and Victim Advocates." *Journal of Interpersonal Violence.* 1(1): 25-42.

Sherman, L. W., and R. A. Berk. 1984. "The Specific Deterrent Effects of Arrest for Domestic Assault." *American Sociological Review.* 49:261-272.

Sherman, L. W., and R. A. Berk. 1984. *The Minneapolis Domestic Violence Experiment.* Washington, DC: Police Foundation.

Smith, D. A. 1987. "Police Response to Interpersonal Violence: Defining the Parameters of Legal Control." *Social Forces.* 65(3): 767-782.

Stephens, D. W. 1977. "Domestic Assault: The Police Response." In M. Roy, ed. *Battered Women: A Psychosociological Study of Domestic Violence.* New York: Van Nostrand Reinhold.

Waaland, P., and S. Keeley. 1985. "Police Decision Making in Wife Abuse: The Impact of Legal and Extralegal Factors." *Law and Human Behavior.* 9(4): 355-366.

Worden, R. E., and A. A. Pollitz. 1984. "Police Arrests in Domestic Disturbances: A Further Look." *Law and Society Review.* 18(1): 105-119.

COURTS AND LEGISLATION

Bolton, F. G., and S. R. Bolton. 1987. "The Legal Environment of Conjugal Violence." In F. G. Bolton and S. R. Bolton, eds. *Victimization Within Families.* Beverly Hills CA: Sage.

Buzawa, E., and C. C. Buzawa. 1985. "Legislative Trends in the Criminal Justice Response to Domestic Violence." In A. J. Lincoln and M. A. Straus, eds. *Crime and the Family.* Springfield, IL: C. C. Thomas.

Carmody, D. C., and K. R. Williams. 1987. "Wife Assault and Perceptions of Sanctions." *Violence and Victims.* 2(1): 25-38.

Field, M. H., and H. F. Field. 1973. "Marital Violence and the Criminal Process: Neither Justice nor Peace." *Social Service Review.* 47(2): 221-240.

Jolin, A. 1983 "Domestic Violence Legislation: An Impact Assessment." *Journal of Police Science and Administration.* 11(4): 451-456.

Lerman, L. 1981. "Criminal Prosecution of Wife Beaters." *Response.* 4(3): 1-5.

Lerman, L. 1981. *Prosecutions of Spouse Abuse: Innovations in Criminal Justice Response.* Washington, DC: Center for Women Policy Studies.

Lerman, L., and F. Livingston. 1983. "State Legislation on Domestic Violence." *Response.* 6(5): 1-6.

National Institute of Justice. 1986. *Confronting Domestic Violence: A Guide for Ciminal Justice Agencies.* Washington, DC: U. S. Dept. of Justice.

Quarm, D., and M. Schwartz. 1983. "Legal Reform and the Criminal Court: The Case of Domestic Violence." Unpublished. University of Cincinnati, OH.

Scales, A. 1986. "The Emergence of Feminist Jurisprudence: An Essay." *Yale Law Journal.* 95(7): 1373-1403.

COMMUNITY SERVICES AND SOCIAL POLICY

Adams, D. 1986. "Wife Abuse Should Be Seen as a Primary Problem, Not a Symptom." *Psychiatric News.* 21(11): 24-29.

Alsdurf, J. M. 1985. "Wife Abuse and the Church: The Response of Pastors." *Response.* 1:9-11.

Barnett, E. R., C. B. Pittman, C. K. Ragan, and M. K. Salus. 1985. *Family Violence: Intervention Strategies.* Washington, DC: GPO.

Borkowski, M., M. Murch, and V. Walker. 1983. *Marital Violence: The Community Response.* New York: Tavistock.

Bowker, L. H. 1983. "Battered Wives, Lawyers, and District Attorneys: An Examination of Law in Action." *Journal of Criminal Justice.* 11(5): 403-412.

Crime Control Institute. 1986. "Police Domestic Violence Policy Change." *Response.* 9(2): 16-18.

Davis, L. 1984. "Beliefs of Service Providers About Abused Women and Abusing Men." *Social Work.* 28(3): 248-250.

Dutton, D. G. 1984. "Interventions into the Problem of Wife Assault: Therapeutic, Policy, and Research Implications." *Canadian Journal of Behavioral Science.* 16(4): 281-297.

Gamache, D., J. Edleson, and M. Schock. 1984. "Coordinated Police, Judicial and Social Service Response to Woman Battering: A Multiple-Baseline Evaluation Across Three Communities." Paper presented at the Second National Conference for Family Violence Researchers, Durham, NH.

Gondolf, E. W. Forthcoming. "Dealing with the Abuser: Issues, Options and Procedures for the Clergy." In A. Horton and J. Williamson, eds. *Abuse and Religion: When Prayer is Not Enough.* Lexington, MA: Lexington.

Goodwin, J. 1985. "Family Violence: Principles of Intervention and Prevention." *Hospital & Community Psychiatry.* 36(10): 1074-1079.

Goolkasian, G. A. 1986. *Confronting Domestic Violence: A Guide for Criminal Justice Agencies.* Washington, DC: GPO.

Lloyd, S., R. Cate, and J. Conger. 1983. "Family Violence and Service Providers: Implications for Training." *Social Casework.* 64(9): 431-435.

Loeb, R. C. 1983. A Program of Community Education for Dealing with Spouse Abuse." *Journal of Community Psychology.* 11(3): 241-252.

Morgan, S. M. 1982. *Conjugal Terrorism: A Psychological and Community Treatment Model of Wife Abuse.* Saratoga, CA: R & E.

Pelton, C. L. 1985. "Family Protection Teams." *Conciliation Courts Review.* 21(1): 87-94.

Roberts, A. R., ed. 1984. *Battered Women and Their Families: Intervention Strategies and Treatment Programs.* New York: Springer.

Sedlak, A. J. 1986. "Prevention of Wife Abuse." In V. B. Van Hasselt, A. S. Bellack, R. L. Morrison, and M. Hersen, eds. *Handbook of Family Violence.* New York: Plenum Press.

Stark, E., A. Flitcraft, and W. Frazier. 1979. "Medicine and Patriarchal Violence: The Social Construction of a 'Private' Event." *International Journal of Health Services.* 9(3): 461-494.

Wodarski, J. S. 1987. "An Examination of Spouse Abuse: Practice Issues for the Professions." *Clinical Social Work Journal.* 15(2): 172-187.

Stone, A. A. 1984. *Law, Psychiatry, and Morality: Essays and Analysis.* Washington, DC: American Psychiatric Press.

Sullivan, G. 1982. "Cooptation of Alternative Services: The Battered Women's Movement as a Case Study." *Catalyst.* 4(2): 39-58.

Wildeman, J., and B. Treen. 1986. "Out of the Kitchen and into the Prison: Towards Sound Social Policy on Domestic Violence." Paper presented at the American Society of Criminology, Atlanta, GA.

Program Resources

— Self-Help Books —

FOR MEN WHO BATTER

Ackerman, R. J. 1987. *Let Go and Grow: Recovery for Adult Children of Alcoholics.* Pompano Beach, FL: Health Communications.

Bach, G., and P. Wyden. 1981. *The Intimate Enemy: How to Fight Fair in Love and Marriage.* New York: Avon.

Benson, H., and M. Klipper. 1976. *Relaxation Response.* New York: Avon.

Brende, J. O., and E. Parsons. 1986. *Vietnam Veterans: The Road to Recovery.* New York: Signet.

Druck, K. 1985. *The Secrets Men Keep: Breaking the Silence Barrier.* Garden City, NY: Doubleday.

Ellis, A. 1977. *How To Live With and Without Anger.* New York: Reader's Digest Press.

Flores, P. 1987. *How to Conquer Your Addiction Through Group Therapy: A Practical Guide to Change Your Addiction Habits with Group Help.* New York: Harrington Park Press.

Gaylin, W. 1980. *Feelings: Our Vital Signs.* New York: Ballantine.

Goffman, M. J. 1980. *Mutual Support Counseling for Woman Batterers.* Redlands, CA: Coalition for the Prevention of Abuse of Women and Children.

Gondolf, E. W., and D. M. Russell. 1987. *Man to Man: A Guide for Men in Abusive Relationships.* Bradenton, FL: Human Services Institute.

Hazelden Foundation. 1987. *Touchstones: A Book of Daily Meditations for Men.* New York: Harper/Hazelden.

Hunt, M., and B. Hunt. 1985. *The Divorce Experience.* New York: Signet.

Jacobs, J., ed. 1986. *Divorce and Fatherhood: The Struggle for Parental Identity.* Washington, DC: American Psychiatric Press.

Julty, S. 1983. *Men's Bodies, Men's Selves.* New York: Delta.

Kiev, Ari. 1982. *How to Keep Love Alive.* New York: Harper & Row.

Lieberman, M., and M. Hardie. 1982. *Resolving Family and Other Conflicts: Everybody Wins.* Santa Cruz, CA: Unity Press.

Miller, S., D. Wackman, E. Nunnally, and C. Saline. 1983. *Straight Talk: A New Way to Get Closer to Others by Saying What You Really Mean*. New York: Signet.

Oakland, T., 1983. *Divorced Fathers: Reconstructing a Quality Life*. New York: Human Sciences Press.

Pietsch, W. 1986. *Human Be-ing: How to Have a Creative Relationship Instead of a Power Struggle*. New York: Signet.

Rosen, G. 1977. *The Relaxation Book: An Illustrated Self-Help Program*. New York: Prentice-Hall.

Ryan, R. S., and J. Travis. 1980. *Wellness Workbook: A Guide to Attaining High Level Wellness*. Berkeley, CA: Ten Speed Press.

Selye, H. 1975. *Stress Without Distress*. New York: Signet.

Walters, R. 1981. *Anger--Yours, Mine and What to Do About It*. Grand Rapids, MI: Zondervan.

Woititz, J. 1983. *Adult Children of Alcoholics*. Pompano Beach: Health Communications.

Zibergeld, B. 1978. *Male Sexuality: A Guide to Sexual Fulfillment*. Boston: Little, Brown.

FOR BATTERED WOMEN

Bowker, L. 1986. *Ending the Violence: A Guidebook Based on the Experiences of One Thousand Battered Wives*. Holmes Beach, FL: Learning Publications.

Forward, S., and J. Torres. 1986. *Men Who Hate Women and the Women Who Love Them*. New York: Bantam.

Hofeller, K. 1983. *Battered Women, Shattered Lives*. Saratoga, CA: R & E.

Isaacs, M. B., B. Montalvo, and D. Abelsohn. 1986. *The Difficult Divorce: Therapy for Children and Families*. New York: Basic Books.

Lerner, H. G. 1986. *The Dance of Anger: A Woman's Guide to Changing the Patterns of Intimate Relationships*. New York: Harper & Row.

McEvoy, A. W., and J. B. Brookings. 1982. *Helping Battered Women: A Volunteer's Handbook for Assisting Victims of Marital Violence*. Holmes Beach, FL: Learning Publications.

NiCarthy, G. 1986. *Getting Free: A Handbook for Women in Abusive Relationships*. Seattle: Seal Press.

NiCarthy, G., K. Merrian, and S. Coffman. 1984. *Talking It Out: A Guide to Groups for Abused Women*. Seattle: Seal Press.

Paris, S., and G. Labinski. 1986. *Mommy and Daddy are Fighting: A Book for Children about Family Violence*. Seattle: Seal Press.

Roberts, A. R. 1981. *Sheltering Battered Women: A National Study and Service Guide*. New York: Springer.

Rouse, L. 1984. *You Are Not Alone: A Guide for Battered Women*. Holmes Beach, FL: Learning Publications.

White, E. 1985. *Chain Chain Change: For Black Women Dealing with Physical and Emotional Abuse*. Seattle: Seal Press.

Zambrano, M. M. 1985. *Mejor Sola Que Mal Acompanada: For the Latina in an Abusive Relationship*. Seattle: Seal Press.

— Program Manuals (Annotated) —

Deschner, J. 1984. *The Hitting Habit: Anger Control for Battering Couples*. New York: Free Press.
A book advocating and outlining anger control treatment for families with spouse and child abuse.

Edleson, J. L., D. Miller, and G. W. Stone. 1985. *Counseling Men Who Batter: Group Leader's Handbook*. Minneapolis: University of Minnesota.
A monograph for social workers leading batterer's groups with special emphasis on group process and facilitation.

EMERGE. 1981. *Organizing and Implementing Services for Men Who Batter*. Boston, MA: EMERGE.
A monograph explaining the assumptions, polices and guidelines for a cooperatively managed, anti-sexist organization for men who batter.

Erickson, E. L., A. W. McEvoy, and N. D. Colucci. 1986. *Child Abuse and Neglect: A Guidebook for Educators and Community Leaders*. Holmes Beach, FL: Learning Publications.
A book of interventions strategies for dealing with cases of child abuse with treatment ideas for the abused child.

Ewing, W., M. Lindsey, and J. Pomerantz. 1984. *Battering: An AMEND Manual for Helpers*. Denver, CO: Littleton Heights College.
A monograph for a batterer's program including procedures and psychosocial exercises from another well established program.

Frank, P., and B. Houghton. 1980. *Confronting the Batterer: A Guidebook to Creating the Spouse Abuse Educational Workshop*. New City, NY: Volunteer Counseling Service.
A monograph outlining a short-term educational program for men who batter focusing on teaching legal and social consequences.

Ganley, A. 1981. *Court Mandated Counseling for Men Who Batter*. Washington, DC: Center for Women Policy Studies.
A training manual of assumptions, assessment, and procedures in conducting court mandated counseling.

Goffman, J. M. 1984. *Batterers Anonymous: Self-Help Counseling for Men Who Batter Women*. San Bernadino, CA: B. A. Press.
A brief outline for setting up a self-help discussion group, similar to Alcoholics Anonymous, for batterers.

Gondolf, E. W. 1985. *Men Who Batter: An Integrated Approach to Stopping Wife Abuse*. Holmes Beach, FL: Learning Publications.
A book of theory, program format, counseling issues, and exercises for anti-sexist, supervised self-help programs.

Hart, B. 1987. *Safety for Women: Monitoring Batterers' Programs*. Harrisburg, PA: Pennsylvania Coalition Against Domestic Violence.
A monograph on how shelters might work with batterer programs to assure safety for women and improve program effectiveness.

Loving, N. 1981. *Spouse Abuse: A Curriculum Guide for Police Trainers*. Washington, DC: Police Executive Research Forum.
A monograph for teaching police wife abuse-related issues.

Mayer, A. 1984. *Incest: A Treatment Manual for Therapy with Victims, Spouses and Offenders*. Holmes Beach, FL: Learning Pubs.
A book of processes for dealing with incest perpetrators.

Mantooth, C. M., R. Geffner, D. Franks, and J. Patrick. 1987. *Family Preservation*. Tyler, TX: Family Preservation.
A program manual for a session-by-session couples program, which features crisis intervention and anger management techniques.

Neidig, P. H., and D. H. Friedman. 1984. *Spouse Abuse: A Treatment Program for Couples.* Champaign, IL: Research Press.
A book of procedures and skill-building exercises for working with violent couples.

RAVEN. 1986. *Safety Planning: RAVEN Phase One Membership Guidebook.* St. Louis, MO: RAVEN.
A workbook for batterers that confronts them with their abuse and teaches how to be more responsible.

Sinclair, D. 1985. *Understanding Wife Assault: A Training Manual for Counsellors & Advocates.* Toronto, Canada: Ontario Government Bookstore.
A counselors manual with conceptual discussion of the social causes of abuse and chapters on group work with battered women, with batterers, and with children.

Sonkin, D., D. Martin, and L. Walker. 1985. *The Male Batterer: A Treatment Approach.* New York: Springer.
A book for therapists outlining the assessment, legal and counseling issues when counseling batterers.

Sonkin, D., and M. Durphy. 1981. *Learning to Live Without Violence.* San Francisco: Volcano Press.
A workbook focusing on controlling anger, dealing with stress, and curbing alcohol abuse.

Star, B. 1983. *Helping the Abuser: Intervening Effectively in Family Violence.* New York: Family Services Association.
A book describing programs for rapists, child abusers, and batterers, and which identifies their common features.

West, L., W. Turner, and E. Dunwoody. 1981. *Wife Abuse in the Armed Services.* Wash. DC: Center for Women Policy Studies.
A monograph explaining wife abuse in the military and a program for military personnel.

— Films —
(To locate films for loan contact your local Library)

WOMAN ABUSE

A Family Affair. VISCOM Productions (28 min).
Documentary drama follows family from battering incident to police action and court proceedings.

Battered Women: Violence Behind Closed Doors. MTI (24 min).
Discussion by battered women (and some men who batter) of the fear and helplessness associated with abuse.

Domestic Violence: The All-American Crime
Task Force on Battered Women (30 min).
Explores the root causes of domestic violence in cultural attitudes and historical violence.

Family Violence in America: The Conspiracy of Violence.
FMS Productions (30 min).
A broad look at domestic violence and how to break its cycle, by victims, abusers, lawyers, service directors, and experts.

Not a Love Story. National Film Board of Canada (68 min).
A film about the many forms of pornography and its acceptance without consideration of the consequences.

Rape/Crisis. The Cinema Guild (87 min).
An award winning docudrama on the roots of sexual violence in our culture.

Rethinking Rape. Film Distribution Center (26 min).
An in-depth look at acquaintance rape and its societal causes.

The Rites of Violence. Minnesota Program Development. (28 min.)
A story about a man who batters his wife and how the community intervenes with a model program of coordinated law enforcement and human services.

The Other Side of Rape. Health Services Consortium
(30 min./ videotape).
A reenactment of a rape scene and the treatment of the victim
to evoke feelings and discussions.

Killing Us Softly: Advertising's Image of Women
Kinetic Film Enterprises. (28 min.)
An eye-opener about the impact of advertising on men's atti-
tudes and behavior toward women.

The Power Pinch. MTI Teleprograms (30 min).
This film critically examines the issue of sexually harassment in
the work place.

Time Out Series: Deck the Halls, Up the Creek, Shifting Gears
ODN Productions (44 min).
Three short dramatizations of violent incidents to stimulate dis-
cussions and self-examination.

To Have and To Hold. New Day Films (25 min).
The first documentary examining the problem of abuse from the
man's experience of it.

We Will Not Be Beaten. Transition House Films (35 min/B&W).
Produced by women in battering relationships. About their
determination to escape battering despite society's neglect.

MEN'S ISSUES

An Acquired Taste. New Day Films (26 min).
A 40-year-old filmmaker's wry look at the school, work, and
media influences that shaped his life. Exposes in particular the
American obsession with being "number one."

Between Men: Masculinity and the Military
United Documentary Films (57 min).
A stunning documentary of the impact of military experience on
men's personal lives.

Growing Up Gay. King Entertainment (30 min/videotape).
A sensitive documentary about four very different young people and their reflections on being homosexual in contemporary America.

Heroes and Strangers. New Day Films (25 min).
In frank conversations, adult sons and daughter's discuss their relationships with their fathers and reflect on its impact on their lives.

Men's Lives. New Day Films (44 min).
A reflection on growing up as a male and the socialization processes that influence us along the way.

New Relations: A Film About Fathers and Sons
Plainsong Productions (30 min).
A documentary of challenges and questions faced by an accepting father; an introduction to changing sex roles and different parenting styles.

Shifting Gears. Mobius International (13 min.).
A powerful drama about wife battering from a man's perspective. Highlights how men can help one another come to terms with abuse.

Stale Roles and Tight Buns. OASIS (23 min).
An audio visual presentation about the stereotyping of American men in advertising.

Up the Creek. Mobius International (15 min.).
A film about the emotional and legal repercussions of wife abuse shown from the man's point of view.

Why Men Rape. Learning Corporation of America (40 min).
Interviews with a variety of convicted rapist on their motivations to rape and underlying power needs.

— Resource Centers —

Center for Women Policy Studies
2000 P St., N.W., Ste. 508, Washington DC 20036
National clearinghouse for information, manuals, legislation related to domestic violence; publishes the *Response* journal.

Ending Men's Violence Task Group
National Organization for Changing Men
c/o Changing Men, PO Box 24159, St. Louis, MO 63130
Representatives from programs dealing with battering and rape, working on public awareness and social action. Co-sponsor of *The Ending Men's Violence National Referral Directory* and the *Ending Men's Violence Newsletter.*

Family Research Laboratory
Dept. of Sociology, University of New Hampshire, Durham, NH 03824
Research center which maintains an extensive bibliography of studies and methodology related to family violence.

Family Violence Research Program
Dept. of Psychology, University of Texas at Tyler, Tyler, TX 75701
Provides a clearinghouse and reference list of research papers related to family violence; publishes *Family Violence Bulletin,* listing new acquisitions.

M.A.R.C. (Men's Anti-rape Resource Center)
Men Stopping Rape, 306 N. Brooks St. Madison, WI 53715
Maintains clearinghouse for instructional and resource materials for programs dealing with rape.

Military Family Resource Center. Toll-free number 800-336-4592.
Provides technical assistance and general information for those working with military families experiencing family problems.

National Woman Abuse Prevention Project
2000 P Street, NW, Ste. 508, Washington, DC 20036
An information and study center focusing on criminal justice intervention in family violence. Publishes *Exchange,* the quarterly newsletter useful to domestic violence workers.

National Clearinghouse on Marital Rape
Women's History Research Center, 2325 Oak St., Berkeley, CA 94708
> Includes access to newsletters, reports, and bibliography on issues of marital rape so often a part of wife abuse.

National Coalition Against Domestic Violence
c/o 1500 Massachusetts Ave, N.W., Suite 35, Washington, DC 20036
> A network of women's shelter programs with a feminist orientation and concern for abuser programs.

NOTE: Most states have statewide coalitions or networks of organizations working against domestic violence which are responsible for public education, lobbying, and fund disbursement.

— Periodicals —

Aegis: Magazine on Ending Violence Against Women
Feminist Alliance Against Rape, P.O. Box 21033, Wash. DC 20009
> A forum for activists examining the roots of violence against women and strategy to end it.

Brother: The News Quarterly of the National Men's Organization
Brother to Brother, 1660 Broad St., Cranston, RI 02905
> A newsletter of short articles, reviews, and resources, on issues related to a movement of changing men (includes task force on ending men's violence).

Changing Men: Issues in Gender, Sex, and Politics
306 North Brook, Madison, WI 53715
> A magazine of essays, short stories and poetry explaining the issues of masculinity in American society.

Exchange: A Forum on Domestic Violence - National Woman Abuse Prevention Project, 2000 P St., NW, #508, Washington, DC 20036
> A quarterly newsletter information, resources, and conferences.

Fact Sheet on Institutional Sexism - Council on Interracial Books for Children, 1841 Broadway, New York, NY 10023.
> A 1982 comparison of men's and women's status in a variety of fields including politics, education, religion, employment.

The Family Violence Bulletin - Family Violence Research Program
University of Texas at Tyler, 3900 University Blvd., Tyler, TX 75701
A quarterly newsletter listing recent papers and publications about family violence.

Journal of Family Violence
Plenum Publishing Corp., 233 Spring St., New York, NY 10013
A journal of research and clinical articles on family violence.

Journal of Interpersonal Violence
Sage Publications, P.O. Box 5024, Beverly Hills, CA 90210
Concerned with the study and treatment of victims and perpetrators of physical and sexual violence.

The Success Network: Newsletter for Non-Profit Executives & Boards
555 Auburn St., Manchester, NH 03103
A monthly newsletter of helpful information on administrative, organizational, funding, and program issues for grassroots and social service organizations.

Passages in Nonviolence: Men for Nonviolence Newsletter
Men for Nonviolence, 1122 Broadway, Fort Wayne, IN 46802
A bi-monthly newsletter of essays, poems, and exercises for dealing with wife abuse and societal violence.

Response (to the victimization of women and children) - Center for Women Policy Studies, 2000 P St., N.W. Suite 508, Wash. DC 20036
A quarterly professional journal reviewing research, books, programs, and legislation in the field of domestic violence and sexual assault.

Victimology: An International Journal
Victimology, Inc., 2333 N. Vernon Street, Arlington, VA 22207
A journal of academic articles on the dynamics of victimization.

Violence and Victims
Springer Publishing, 536 Broadway, New York, NY 10012
Journal of research articles on victimization and wife abuse.

— Reference Books —

Alcohol and the Family: A Comprehensive Bibliography, by G. M. Barnes and D. K. Augustino, 1987. Westport, CN: Greenwood.
   A bibliography of research, treatment and family issues.

Battered Women's Directory, 9th ed., by B. Warrior, 1985. Boston: Warrior Press.
   A comprehensive directory of shelter services and other aids for battered women.

The Ending Men's Violence National Referral Directory, by RAVEN, 1986. RAVEN, P.O. Box 24159, St. Louis, MO 63130.
   A directory listing over 300 programs for men who batter or rape.

How and Where to Research and Find Information About Child Abuse, by R. D. Reed, 1983. Saratoga, CA: R & E.
   A guide to organizations, bibliographies, magazine articles and newsletters dealing with child abuse.

The Male Sex Role: A Selected and Annotated Bibliography, by K. E. Grady, R. Brannon, and J. H. Pleck, 1979. Washington, DC: GPO.
   A comprehensive listing of research articles related to sex role socialization and its impact.

Sheltering Battered Women: A National Survey and Service Guide, by A. Roberts, 1981. New York: Springer.
   An overview of shelter services available in the U.S.; partial directory.

Spouse Abuse: An Annotated Bibliography of Violence Between Mates, by E. A. Engeldinger, 1986. Metuchen, NJ: Scarecrow Press.
   A list of research articles and books on studies of wife abuse through 1983.

Violence in the Family: An Annotated Bibliography, by E. Kemmer, 1984. New York: Garland.
   A bibliography (through 1982) on wife, child and elder abuse including 1,000 entries from practitioners and researchers.

AUTHOR INDEX

Abbott, F. 30
Abelsohn, D. 75
Abrams, W. 54
Ackerman, R. J. 49,50,74
Adams, D. 10,45,57,71
Adesso, V. J. 50
Aiken, P. A. 60
Albritten, W. L. 24
Albritten-Bogal, R. B. 24
Alder, E. M. 20
Allen, C. M. 20,23
Alsdurf, J. M. 71
Alter-Reid, K. 47
Alwin, D. F. 36
Amato, P. R. 23
Andersen, S. M. 26
Anderson, C. 55
Anderson, J. 55
Andrews, F. 31
Araji, S. 47
Arbitell, M. 21
Arcana, J. 33
Arias, I. 24,65
Armstrong, L. 11,15
Ashmore, R. D. 29
Astrachan, A. 5,33
Atkinson, J. 29
Austin, G. 70
Averill, J. 38

Bach, G. 74
Bagarozzi, D. 18
Balgopal, P. R. 53
Ball, M. 60
Ball-Rokeach, S. J. 40
Balswick, J. O. 36
Bandura, A. 39
Barboru, L. S. 27
Bard, M. 49
Barling, J. 23,65
Barnett, E. R. 71
Barnett, O. W. 42,44
Barnum, R. 49
Barrett, M. J. 48
Barshis, V. C. 46
Bart, P. 22
Bartal, D. 26
Baucom, D. H. 60,65
Baumli, F. 5,33
Beach, S. R. 65
Beauvis, C. 64
Beck, A. T. 55,65
Bedrosian, R. C. 61

Beeman, M. S. 64
Bell, D. 31,69
Bellack, A. S. 50, 56,72
Bem, S. L. 65
Benke, T. 48
Benson, H. 74
Benson, M. 52
Berghorn, G. 61
Berk, R. 11,17,26, 69,70
Berk, S. F. 17,26, 29,69
Berkowitz, L. 38, 39,40
Berliner, L. 47
Berman, J. S. 57
Bern, E. H. 17,23, 45,49,58
Bern, L. L. 58
Bernard, J. L. 2,3, 19,24,28,45
Bernard, M. L. 2,3, 19,24,45
Bernard, S. L. 24
Bertcher, H. J. 53
Bess, B. 32
Biaggio, M. K. 36
Biderman, A. D. 65
Bidwell, L. 46
Biernacki, P. 52
Billingham, R. E. 24
Bishop, G. V. 47
Bissell, L. 51
Blackie, S. 60
Blanchard, D. C. 39
Blanchard, R. J. 39
Blane, H. T. 8,51
Blasi, A. 55
Blos, P. 31
Blumenthal, M. 31
Blumstein, P. 29
Blythe, B. J. 68
Bograd, M. 7,16,21, 41,45,56,57,61
Bohmer, S. 56
Bolman, S. R. 19
Bologh, R. W. 45
Bolton, F. G. 42,61,71
Bolton, S. R. 42,61,71
Bond, C. F. 50
Bordin, E. S. 9,67
Borkowski, M. 72
Boulette, T. R. 26
Bowen, N. H. 56

Bower, A. M. 65
Bowker, L. 1,2,10,15, 20,21,26,46,69, 72,75
Boyd, V. 58
Brandell, J. R. 55
Brannon, R. 33,37
Breines, W. 3,7,18
Brekke, J. S. 65
Brende, J. O. 74
Brennan, A. F. 57
Brennan, T. 60
Briar, S. 68
Briere, J. 24
Brockopp, K. 26
Brod, H. 31
Bromet, E. 50
Brookings, J. B. 75
Brothers, J. 31
Brown, J. 67
Browne, A. 15,18
Brownell, A. 9,36,53
Browning, J. J. 43, 62,65
Brownmiller, S. 28,48
Brutz, J. L. 23
Brygger, M. P. 58, 63,67
Buckley, L. B. 61
Burge, S. K. 48
Burger, A. L. 29
Burkhart, B. R. 25
Burkhart, R. R. 26
Burnett, E. C. 35
Butler, K. E. 44
Buzawa, C. C. 71
Buzawa, E. 71
Byles, J. A. 50

Cahn, T. 66
Cahn, T. S. 43
Callaghan-Chaffee, M. E. 23
Camburn, D. 36
Campbell, A. 40
Campbell, J. L. 50
Campell, J. C. 21
Cane, R. M. 59
Cantoni, L. 61
Caplan, P. 45
Carlson, B. 41
Carlson, B. E. 17,25
Carmody, D. C. 71
Carr, J. 69
Carrillo, T. P. 25,43

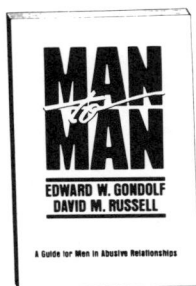

A Guide for Men in Abusive Relationships

Man to Man speaks frankly to men in abusive relationships. This is the kind of book that a man can give to a friend in need, a wife can give her husband, or that an alcohol counselor can make available to a client. Using real-life examples of how abuse occurs and progresses in relationships, *Man to Man* offers the lessons learned by abusive men who have changed. It tells of the consequences of abuse, how to find help and how to stop.

Man to Man helps the reader improve old relationships and develop new, positive ones. It is not a quick-fix book nor a book on marriage treatment—but it provides valuable guidance for lasting change. It clearly presents the commitment and time required to change. And it is written with a recognition that some relationships or marriages are beyond saving once abuse arises.

B012 (Softcover) $ 4.95

ORDER FORM

_B012_	___	_Man to Man, A Guide_	_$ 4.95_

SUB-TOTAL: _____

Florida Residents add 5% Sales Tax: _____

PLEASE ADD NECESSARY SHIPPING & HANDLING: _____
1-2 items, $2.75 ● 3-5 items, $3.50 ● 6 or more, $5.00

TOTAL AMOUNT THIS ORDER: _____

PLEASE PRINT

Name_____

Institution_____

Street_____

City_____ State_____

Zip_____ Phone (_____) _____

To order call (813) 746-7088 or Mail orders to:

HUMAN SERVICES INSTITUTE, P.O. Box 14610, Bradenton, FL 34280